GETTING STARTED IN
ADULT RELIGIOUS EDUCATION

Getting Started in Adult Religious Education

A Practical Guide

JAMES J. DEBOY JR.

PAULIST PRESS
New York/Ramsey/Toronto

Library of Congress
Catalog Card Number: 79–88932

ISBN: 0–8091–2222–7

Published by Paulist Press
Editoral Office: 1865 Broadway, New York, N.Y. 10023
Business Office: 545 Island Road, Ramsey, N.J. 07446

Printed and bound in the
United States of America

Contents

Acknowledgements

I am indebted to many persons who were most generous in assisting with the preparation of this book. The first two drafts of this work were done while the author was Coordinator of Adult Religious Education for the Catholic Diocese of Richmond, Virginia. I am especially appreciative to Bishop Walter F. Sullivan who strongly promoted the development of adult education programs throughout the Diocese of Richmond and encouraged me in my work with adult education committees, parish councils and diocesan collegial bodies while I was a member of his staff from 1975 to 1978.

I also owe special thanks to all those throughout the Diocese of Richmond who reacted to the first draft which was circulated throughout the Diocese of Richmond in the fall of 1976. The following people contributed greatly to the work through their written reactions: Sister Marie Chiodo, D. W., Brother Cosmas Rubencamp, C. F. X., Mary Margaret Swogger, Cathleen Hosey, Sister Mary Grace, O. P., Bob Bulle, Bob Hudy, Nelda Stine, William J. O'Brien, Reverend Paul Meier, Ceal Donohue, Sister Eileen Fitzgerald, Sister Katharine Hanrahan, S. C. N., Sally J. Barry, Sister Marie Vianney, C. S. C., Sister M. Beniti, C. S. C., David Riley, the Christian Formation Committee-Church of the Ascension, Mildred Willis, Brother Philip Dougherty, C. F. X., John J. Harrington, Sister Mary Christine Zindel, M. S. B. T. and Sister Stephanie Bennett.

The following persons also offered critiques and reactions to the first draft: Thomas J. Tewey, Reverend Gorman Sullivan, O. Carm., Reverend Jack Welch, O. Carm., and William Dalglish.

I am also especially grateful to the Staff of the Office of Christian Education in the Diocese of Richmond for their encouragement, interest and helpful suggestions. They provided the stimulus to begin this work and the on-going critique that helped keep me honest and on target: Sister Lourdes Sheehan, R. S. M., Cris Villapando, John Roberto, Donald Howard, S. A., Clarisse Croteau-Chonka, Sister Elaine McCarron, S. C. N., Sister Anna Neuland, C. S. C., Sister Emily Ann Appleton, S. C. N., Reverend J. Stephen O'Brien, who first suggested that I seek a publisher, and Edward J. Murray, whose close friendship and daily challenges while driving together to work and workshops provided the continual support necessary to complete the second draft.

This work reached publication status through the careful efforts of Barbara Reardon, Rachel Hopps, Chris Zinkand and Rosalie Heaney, who typed the several versions with patience, and Stephen Chovanec, who did the art work in the second draft.

Two particular persons in the Archdiocese of Baltimore merit special attention: Reverend James R. Shaefer has been a constant source of encouragement from my first involvement as an adult educator in helping to pilot the GIFT Program and who carefully critiqued the first draft and assisted me in seeking a publisher; H. Richard McCord has been a thorough and encouraging evaluator of both the first and second drafts and a most supportive colleague in the Department of Education in the Archdiocese of Baltimore. Both have ably demonstrated their expertise as adult educators, and I am deeply grateful for their excellent assistance and encouragement.

Finally, I am deeply grateful to those persons who have helped me most in my own growth as an adult believer, Mary and Jim DeBoy, my deeply believing and loving parents, and Peggy, John and Mark whose daily love and support make growth possible and enjoyable.

Introduction

This book has been written to fill a specific need—how *to get started* in developing an effective program for adult religious education at the local level. It is intended to be a basic and introductory resource for those responsible for and involved in planning and implementing adult religious education programs.

Today there is a vast amount of material available about the theory and practice of adult religious education. As a diocesan coordinator of adult religious education, I experienced many occasions when people expressed the desire to find out what issues and topics they would need to address in becoming involved in adult religious education. In responding to this desire, I was challenged to find those specific resources that would give people an accurate picture without overwhelming them. I looked for one introductory resource that I could give to adult education committees and other interested persons to read and study in the process of deciding whether or not they wanted to become involved in planning programs for adults. After working for a year at the diocesan level, I found no satisfactory introductory resource. So with the encouagement of colleagues, I decided to write a book to meet the need I had discovered.

In preparing to do the book, I decided to use a process that would be in accord with the principles of adult learning. So I consulted with a small group of people to determine the

1

topics that should be included in the book. Then I wrote an initial draft which was circulated to pastors, professional religious educators (parish DRE's and diocesan staff personnel), and volunteer adult education chairpersons for their reactions and suggestions for improvement.

After receiving numerous reactions, the book was significantly rewritten and expanded to include the suggestions and additional topics which emerged from the consultation. This publication represents a minor revision and expansion of that second draft.

Those who have been involved in the planning and implementation of programs for adult religious education will find much in this work that is familiar to them. However, these experienced persons may find the book to be useful as a quick overview and a helpful tool in initiating new persons into the process of planning and implementing adult religious education programs.

A thorough consideration of this book should insure that the basic issues and concerns regarding adult religious education are discussed. The book is arranged in a format that addresses the questions and concerns I most frequently encountered in my work in adult education. Local individual planning teams and committees can use this resource as an initial step in developing programs for adults. Questions are provided after each chapter to stimulate further learning and to explore the implications of the major concerns discussed in the chapter. Additional resources will have to be consulted. Many issues presented here in an introductory way will have to be developed further.

As an aid to individuals or groups in deciding which parts of this book can be of most immediate use, a self-assessment is provided to enable persons to determine which particular topics they feel they want to learn about most quickly.

As stated earlier, this book is intended as an introductory tool and not the final word. All those who use it are encour-

1.
What Is Adult
Religious Education?

Many Church leaders and statements say "it" is the central process for a vibrant Church. More and more people are expressing an interest in pursuing "it." More and more resources are being published to help people do "it." But there is still lots of confusion about what "it" is. "It" is adult religious education.

To describe adult religious education clearly, it is necessary to make some distinctions between and among *adult learning, adult education* and *schooling.*

Adult learning is happening all the time. Adults learn by talking with neighbors, listening to the radio or watching TV, reading the newspaper, doing one's job, participating in community activities, overhearing conversations at the barber shop or beauty parlor, and many other ways. Much learning occurs through accidental and surprising ways. One can be taken suddenly ill and be rushed to the hospital and learn a great deal about the uncertainty of life and our dependency on others. Learning is happening constantly.

Schooling is one structured, yet comprehensive, approach to learning. Because of various laws as well as the necessities of life, just about everyone has had an extensive experience of schooling. In the minds of many people, schooling is associated with teachers, desks, books, buildings, bells, homework, grades and graduation. Some recall their experiences of schooling as growthful, positive, enjoyable, enriching and essentially necessary to their success in life. But others, perhaps because of poor grades, failures or punishments, look upon their schooling as a negative, regressive, unpleasant and not very helpful experience in their life.

Many people tend to view schooling in a uniform way—that everyone's experience of schooling is generally the same, with some possible variation in an individual's success in school. But this tendency does not reflect the many different approaches that are possible in schools, nor does it reflect the fact that the processes of schooling have been, and continue to be, changing and developing. The experiences people are having in schools today are quite different from those who graduated from elementary school twenty-five years ago. Even the educational approach called schooling has undergone many changes.

It seems to be true that many people tend to react to programs for adult education in much the same way that they reacted to their schooling. This tendency blurs the distinction between adult education and schooling. If "school" meant memorizing and fear of being "called on," then someone who associates adult religious education with his/her experience of schooling will avoid adult religious education because "the speaker might call on me."

What then is *adult education*? It is not the same as adult learning, nor is it the same as schooling, but it is related to both. Adult education is an intentional effort to provide learning opportunities for adults. While adult learning can often be accidental, adult education is planned. While schooling is an extended process that is comprehensive and intensive, adult education may be very specific and short-term in one area of life and longer and more intensive in another.

Now it is appropriate to attempt a definition of adult

religious education. However, in order to do so, it is necessary to consider several elements.

Adult religious education is *planned*. It is not haphazard or accidental. Adult religious education is the result of people working together to provide activities which will enable adults to gain an insight into their spiritual needs, to examine previous formed attitudes and theories, to see others practicing a faith life and to experience a faith growth themselves.

Adult religious education strives to *foster adult learning*. There is no guarantee that adults will actually learn through participation in adult religious education programs. Just as with schooling, mere presence is not a guarantee that learning will take place. But adult religious education programs should be planned according to principles of adult learning which maximize the probability that adults will learn.

Adult religious education is for *adults*, and it is therefore necessary for planners and leaders to understand the needs of adults and the adult stages of psychological and faith development. There are approaches that are more appropriate for children than adults and vice versa. A chronological age is only one factor in determining whether one is truly an adult.

Adult religious education strives to *awaken and deepen* one's *faith*. Faith can be awakened or deepened through concern for content (e.g., doctrine, history, theology), actions (ways of worship, witnessing to one's faith, nurturing the faith of others) and intent or purpose (to help people be better parents, spouses, members of the community or more fulfilled individuals). Therefore, adult religious education is concerned with knowledge, understanding and daily living. It is not enough to "know" that there are seven sacraments. Adult believers need to understand the meaning of the sacraments and live this meaning every day.

These elements of adult religious education will be further developed in the remaining chapters of this book. In light of what has been said, the following is suggested as a working definition of "adult religious education" as it is used in this book: "Adult religious education is the planned effort to provide opportunities to enable adults to awaken or deepen their knowledge, understanding and daily living of their faith."

No definition is ever totally adequate. This definition is presented to indicate what is meant by *adult religious education* when used in this book. Adult religious education is not merely "whatever we do with adults"—even though the principles of adult learning should apply whenever adults gather. Those who are prompted to continue reading should be aware that the remaining chapters of this book will attempt to explain and develop the meaning of adult religious education in accord with the definition presented here.

Questions To Consider

   A. What is your own personal definition of "adult religious education"?
   B. How does your definition differ from the one presented in this chapter?
   C. What elements would you add or omit from this definition?

Additional Learning Resources

   Adult Religious Education, Leon McKenzie, Twenty-Third Publications, P.O. Box 180, West Mystic, Conn. 06388, 1975. (Paper, 8½ x 11, 160 pp.) In Chapter 1, the author develops a definition of adult religious education which is broader than the one presented here.

   The Church as Reflecting Community: Models of Adult Religious Learning, Loretta Girzaitis, Twenty-Third Publications, P.O. Box 180, West Mystic, Conn. 06388, 1977. (Paper, 8½ x 11, 186 pp.) Chapter 2 describes adult religious growth and the dimensions of the term "religious education."

"What Is Religious Education?" Charles F. Melchert, *The Living Light*, Vol. 14, No. 3, Fall 1977, pp. 339-352. Melchert prompts the reader to clarify what is meant by "education," "religion" and "religious education." Though not directed specifically to adult religious education, this article and the response to it (following immediately) by John Westerhoff are very stimulating and challenging.

2.
Why Have Adult Religious Education?

It is fashionable in religious education circles to say: "Adult education is our number one priority." Parish leaders and committees often make that remark. Church authorities and documents have also stressed the importance of adult education. For example the Sacred Congregation of the Clergy said in the *General Catechetical Directory:* "They [shepherds of souls] should also remember that catechesis for adults, since it deals with persons who are capable of an adherence that is fully responsible, must be considered the chief form of catechesis. All other forms, which are indeed always necessary, are in some way oriented to it" (n. 20).

The American bishops in their pastoral message on Catholic education entitled, *To Teach As Jesus Did*, said: "Consequently the continuing education of adults is situated not at the periphery of the Church's educational mission but at its center" (n. 43). They later added: "The full content of revelation can be communicated best to those able by reason of maturity and prior preparation to hear and respond to it. Religious education for adults is the culmination of the entire catechetical effort because it affords an opportunity to teach the whole Christian message" (n. 47).

The American bishops spoke strongly again about adult

11

religious education in *Sharing the Light of Faith*, their recently published National Catechetical Directory: "Because of its importance and because all other forms of catechesis are oriented in some way to it, the catechesis of adults must have high priority at all levels of the Church. The success of programs for children and youth depends to a significant extent upon the words, attitudes, and action of the adult community, especially parents, family and guardians" (n. 188).

Despite these statements by Church authorities and those involved in religious education, the question is still asked: "Why is adult education so important? If we do a good job teaching the youth, the adults ought to be able to take care of themselves." To respond to this adequately, it is necessary to examine further what we mean by religion and education.

For many Catholics, religion is frequently associated with the acceptance of a certain body of doctrine and compliance with specific laws. However, religion is much more involved with *relationships*: our relationship with God, with the others who believe in him, and with all those who have never even heard of God. Doctrine and laws are important aspects of growing in our relationships with God and others, but not the most important. A person can accept a certain doctrine as true without ever entering into a personal relationship with the Father, through Jesus in the Spirit, which is the core of Christian faith. A religious response involves one's total life and not just certain aspects of one's life nor just certain days of one's life.

Education is often seen as the acquisition of knowledge and skills. This is part of education, but the major thrust of education is to enable one to reach full potential as a person in relationship with other persons. Education is not something that is poured into someone from the outside. It is also an internal process which can be facilitated or hindered by outside influences and structures. Education is an orderly and systematic approach to facilitate a person's growth toward maturity.

If considered in these ways, both religion and education are dynamic, not static, processes. If religion were only the acceptance of doctrine and the compliance with laws, it might be possible to "learn enough to get by," or reach a point where it is possible to say: "I know all I need to know." But because religion is a dynamic relationship—with Jesus and other persons—it is never possible to say: "I've had enough."

Adult religious education is especially important because only adults are fully able to enter into relationships. Moreover, our relationships can always be deepened and renewed. Thus, for both individual and community reasons, adult education is essential.

Individual Reasons for Adult Religious Education

Adult religious education is important for reasons arising from the nature, qualities and responsibilities of an individual person. Among these "individual reasons" are the following: the nature of persons, the stages of adult development, the nature of faith, fulfilling our roles in life, and the nature of the world. Each of these reasons will be explained further in paragraphs that follow.

The Nature of Persons

Every person is a unique individual who can never be fully understood or known. A clear example of this is the relationship between husband and wife or between two best friends. There never is a time when one can truthfully say, "I know you as well as I'll ever know you." Indeed, if this is actually said (or thought), that is the time when the relationship is beginning to deteriorate because the persons take each other for granted. If this is true for human persons who can see, hear and touch one another, how much more true is it for God. Thus, there is never a time when we can legitimately say, "I know all there is to know about God." We can always learn more and more about God and our relationship with God.

The Stages of Adult Development

At one time, adulthood was considered to be a state that one reached at a certain age and there was really not much further growth (except in waistline). We now know through much reflection and research that adults go through many stages of development. Chapter 4 will provide an expanded explanation of the stages of adult development. If adults do experience stages, then a religious commitment made at one stage of development must be renewed and deepened after the person has moved to a later stage, or the commitment will gradually fade and die. Because adults are changing persons, commitments cannot be made just once and for all. Rather, to stay alive, commitments must be continually renewed and deepened.

The Nature of Faith

Faith is a dynamic relationship which is continually changing. A faith relationship between two or more persons is not a static thing. It will not remain the same, even if left alone, but rather will stagnate like water in a still pool. Faith is not just an intellectual assent to certain principles. Faith involves our whole being—the way we think, know, feel, and act.

We must strive to deepen and update our faith relationships so that they will remain vibrant. Many of us have had the experience of moving away from a very good friend who meant a lot to us and then have the friendship gradually fade away for one reason or another because we did not stay in touch and keep the friendship alive. It is likewise important that we continually update and deepen our relationship with

14

Jesus if our friendship with him is to stay alive and grow.

Chapter 5 will deal with stages of faith development. Since faith is a developing experience, on-going efforts to grow and expand in faith are vitally important for adults—if faith is to remain alive.

Fulfilling Our Roles in Life

Each of us has certain roles in life. We are friend, spouse, parent, worker, etc. We have also accepted the role of *believer* if we have made a commitment to Jesus through the Church. Being *a believer* ought to influence our response in every other role we fulfill. To fulfill our roles successfully, we need to know and understand the responsibilities of those roles and use the necessary skills to effectively carry out the responsibilities of being spouse, parent, friend, or worker. Since all these roles involve relationships, we can never say we have learned enough to fulfill them perfectly. We can always be more effective. Though we would rarely, if ever, say that we have learned our job well enough to do it perfectly, we often have fallen into this kind of attitude in other roles in life. Being willing to learn more and more is necessary to effectively carry out our roles in life—especially the role of believer. The specific skills needed to be an active believer are discussed below in the section on the mission of the Church.

The Nature of the World

We live in a world that is constantly changing. We have to deal with complexities of living that our grandparents never even imagined. In order to integrate the message of the Gospel with our daily life, it is necessary to reflect continually on the Gospel and its richness to discover its meaning in today's world. It would be nice to be able to turn the clock back and not have to face crucial issues like test-tube babies, nuclear proliferation and other problems brought about by the advancement of science. We can't turn away. It is our challenge to respond to these problems in the light of the Gospel. Ignoring them won't make them go away. To deal with these issues, we have to deepen our understanding of the Gospel (a lifelong task in itself) and try as best we can to understand the world we live in.

Community Reasons for Adult Religious Education

Because we belong to a community of persons who believe in God and commit themselves to Jesus in his Spirit and strive to share his message with others, there are community reasons for adult religious education. Some of these "community reasons" are: the mission of a parish, the nature of the Church, and the need for an active adult community.

The Mission of a Parish

The purpose of a parish is to develop a community of *believing persons* who *do* the following: (1) celebrate their beliefs in active *worship* of God, (2) strive to *witness* to their beliefs through active *service* to the world, and (3) try to enable all the members of the community to *grow* in their relationship with Jesus and with one another—in other words, the *nurturing* of its members. This threefold mission of worship, witness/service, and nurture are all interrelated. The following illustration may be helpful in understanding the interrelationship:

16

Worship and witness/service are worthy goals in themselves. It is good to worship the Lord, and to witness to what we believe by serving others. Moreover, good worship should lead people to more active efforts to witness and serve. And effective witness and service should lead people to worship. The element of nurture is foundational because it enables persons to grow to achieve their fullest possible potential, and it enables them to worship and witness and serve more effectively. Good worship also promotes personal growth and effective witness and service stimulates further growth.

On-going religious education is vitally important in enabling a community to achieve the threefold mission of a parish. Effective religious education enables people to understand and participate actively in worship experiences. Religious education enables people to realize that service to others is a fundamental element of the Gospel of Christ, and it also enables people to determine areas of need and the appropriate actions to take to respond to these needs. And religious education fosters personal growth in each individual in the process of maturing as a believer. To fulfill effectively the mission of a parish, a community must continually strive to improve its understanding and living of the Gospel.

The Nature of the Church

The documents of Vatican Council II suggest several images for the Church. One of the most important of these images is the Church as the pilgrim people of God. This image clearly shows those aspects of the Church through which it is ever growing, ever changing, because it is composed of changing, growing persons. Within the Church, there are many roles, and at this time in Church history we are rediscovering these ministries. Fifteen years ago, the priest did practically everything in our worship. At times he needed ushers and altar boys. Now we have rediscovered and implemented the roles of lector, cantor, and special minister of the Eucharist. We also have

17

parish councils, with liturgy, social ministry, education and administration committees. These rediscovered ministries within the Church are vitally important to the life of the Church—they are not just "nice to have around." Those involved in these ministries must understand and perform them effectively. Those of us who are served by these ministries must also understand them to fully appreciate them. Ongoing education is needed by those who fulfill these ministries and by those who are served by them if the life of the Church is to develop more fully. Those who strive to be adult believers are called to share in these roles.

Moreover, the Church is in the process of renewing and reviving its sacramental life. All the sacramental rites have been revised to make them more understandable and vital to us today. Many changes have occurred and many more will come. People over thirty who have not made a strong effort to update their knowledge of the Church and its sacramental life probably find today's Church unrecognizable and very uncomfortable. Such a person is probably operating out of a model of the Church which no longer exists. The basic truths have not changed, but the terminology and mode of expression have changed a great deal. Words like "ministry," "witness" and "community" were rarely heard ten or fifteen years ago. Now they are heard all the time. If we are to understand and live the meaning of these words, there is a need for education which is oriented toward personal renewal.

The Need for an Active Adult Community

In the past, it was often the case that we expected more from the youth in the Church than we did from the adults. People became upset if teenagers leaned against the wall in the back of the church. Not too much, if anything, was said about the adults who did the same thing—or pushed to get into the very last pew to get an early start out of the church. But, whether they realize it or not, the adults are the most effective

18

teachers in the Church community. Youth want to be like the adults. If they perceive that being an adult in the Church means standing in the back, rushing for the last pew, not responding at worship, complaining about changes, etc., that's what they'll do. For good or ill, the adult community is the most influential factor in the education of the youth in every community. So, if we want youth to be involved actively in the life of the Church, there must be, as a minimum, a vibrant adult community to lead them and provide them with models to imitate.

Moreover, the Church depends largely on the lay members of the community to carry the message of the Gospel to the world. Priests and religious can't go everywhere and do everything. To make the message of Jesus known, the lay members of the community need to know and live the message well and also acquire and use the necessary skills to proclaim the message effectively. If the Gospel is to be lived and proclaimed throughout the world, it must largely be done by knowledgeable, active and deeply committed lay persons who know what they are about.

For these reasons, the Church needs, and just doesn't hope for, a knowledgeable and involved adult community. Within such a community, there is a continuing and vital need for on-going education among the adults. Without it, the Gospel will not be proclaimed and the Church will not fulfill its mission.

What happens if we don't have knowledgeable and involved adult believers?

If there exists within the Church an attitude that it is possible to "get by" with a certain level of knowledge and it is possible to remain on a certain plateau of faith commitment, then the level of faith involvement will gradually begin to decay. The interest and participation in worship will fade away. The effort to witness and serve will disintegrate. Youth will imitate the adults and become disinterested and uninvolved. The parish will not effectively fulfill its mission. This is what happens, has happened, and still is happening in some places where we say: "We have enough adult education."

The Church cannot be a viable community without growing, developing, sharing, and concerned members who are continually striving to deepen their faith through greater knowledge and more vibrant living. When there is no effective effort for continuing adult education within the community, the entire community teaches very loudly and clearly: "Religion is just for kids." If we don't want this to happen, we have to continually strive to improve and expand our efforts in adult religious education. When it comes to adult religious education, we must be convinced that *there is never enough*.

Questions To Consider

    A. What other reasons are there why adult religious education is important?

    B. Which of the reasons given here relates best to your own local community?

    C. What are the possible responses people could give to counter the reasons suggested in this chapter?

Additional Resource

The Church as Reflecting Community: Models of Adult Religious Learning, Loretta Girzaitis, Twenty-Third Publications, P.O. Box 180, West Mystic, Conn. 06388, 1977. (Paper, 8½ x 11, 186 pp.) Chapter 1 discusses the need for continuing learning, and Chapter 5 discusses the role of the community as educator.

3.
Who Is
An Adult?

Adulthood has often been associated with reaching a certain age. We have to pay adult prices at movies and amusement parks when we reach thirteen. We can register to vote and get a marriage license at eighteen. In some states alcoholic beverages can be purchased by those who are eighteen and in other states only by those who are twenty-one. Many people consider someone to be an adult when one or other of these ages is reached. Although persons who reach their majority are expected to act responsibly, we know that often they do not and cannot act as responsible individuals.

On the other hand, some youngsters only nine or ten years old in poor sections of large cities take full responsibility for themselves as well as others. Though their quality of life may be low and their methods may not be conventional, these youngsters find their own shelter, acquire food and clothing and make major decisions regarding their life without assistance or guidance from anyone. These youngsters have been forced to assume much more responsibilty for their lives than many persons three or four times their age.

If being an adult does not depend on chronological age, what are the criteria for determining adulthood? Some suggested criteria for determining whether someone is an adult follow.

An adult is one who faces up to the issues and problems of life by being informed about these issues. The mature person examines the possible consequences and outcomes of decisions *before* making them, often seeking advice from others in the process of facing problems and making decisions. An adult decides and lives with the consequences and responsibilities of that decision. Ordinarily one has to live more than a few years to be able to respond as an adult, but age alone does not guarantee it.

It is a characteristic of children to make decisions without considering the possible consequences, and then when the outcome is uncomfortable or unpleasant, they attempt to shift responsibility to someone else.

An adult sees that most situations in life involve varying degrees of complexity. For the adult the world is not cut and dried or black and white. Instead, it is composed of many shades of gray. The world of children is black and white—answers are simple and neat—and there has to be an answer to every question. An adult realizes that most questions in life are complicated and some problems have no final solution this side of heaven. Adults are vitally aware that change is an essential reality of life.

An adult realizes that there is an interaction with and dependence on others. This mutual inter-dependence is seen as necessary, and one's decisions must take into account the effects they will have on others. The adult is, therefore, mutually responsible and accountable to others.

Additionally, an adult can set aside his or her own needs temporarily to respond to the needs of others. The willingness to serve others is a mark of human and religious maturity.

Thus, a person growing toward adulthood is a self-directing person who makes informed decisions and accepts the consequences of them. As an adult, the individual accepts responsibility for mistakes and understands the need to say, "I'm sorry."

A person is an adult whenever he or she responds and behaves in the above ways. Some people are adults at an early age; others show signs of immaturity all their lives. It is possible, however, to respond as an adult in some areas of life, such as business, and respond as a child in other areas of life, for example, in marriage and religion. It is not uncommon for persons to exercise great responsibility in one area of their life and to neglect other areas.

The Adult Believer

Because Christian life involves a commitment to the person of Jesus and a commitment to other persons, only an adult fully possesses the necessary aptitudes and capacities to make such a commitment. An adult believer understands and accepts the tremendous challenge presented by Jesus to those who would be his followers. Jesus challenges his followers: "Love your enemies, do good to those who hate you, bless those who curse you, and pray for those who mistreat you" (Luke 6:27-28). Jesus commands his followers: "Love one another—just as I love you. The greatest love one can have for one's friends is to give one's life for them. And you are my friends if you do what I command" (John 15:12-14).

An adult believer appreciates the difficulty and consequences of making a commitment to live as a follower of Jesus. An adult believer realizes the need to depend on and support others in living the message of Jesus. An adult believer realizes that one is never "finished" or "completed" in the effort to live the message of Jesus. The adult believer sees the Church as a community of persons who are trying to understand the message of Jesus more clearly and live it more fully. For the adult believer, the Church is not a club to belong to or an answer machine for life's questions and problems. For the adult, the Church is a community of persons who strengthen and support one another by proclaiming the kingdom of the

Lord until he comes again. The adult believer realizes that each person has unique talents and gifts which are necessary for the growth of the community and that each person is responsible for growing continually as an involved member of the community.

In the Church, there are many persons at many levels of awareness of what it means to be an adult believer. It is the responsibility of the entire Church community to help each person grow in an understanding and realization of what it means to be an adult Christian as he or she experiences the many changes in adult life.

We—Not They

Frequently many of us who are involved in adult religious education fall into the habit of thinking and speaking about how we can make "them" grow as adult believers. But the reality is that when we are talking about adult religious education, we are talking about "us." Adult education is not something "we" do for "them." Rather adult education is something "we're all in together." We all need to grow in our relationship with Jesus and with one another.

To become more aware of the challenge, opportunities and needs involved in developing effective learning programs for adults, look carefully at the worshiping community gathered at your Sunday eucharistic celebration. Who is present? There are usually lots of children. In addition to the children, there are many others at various stages of adulthood. Could this be a cross section of your worshiping community?

Teenagers: who are searching into the meaning of life and challenging adults about what they believe and why.

Singles: who are in the process of making or living decisions regarding career choices, vocations, finding meaningful relationships.

Engaged couples and those preparing for marriage: who are establishing and deepening their relationships with each other and looking forward to their life together.

24

Newly marrieds: who are experiencing the joys and tensions of married life.

New parents: who are responding to the added responsibilities of caring for new members of the community.

Parents of teenagers: who must deal every day with the challenges and tensions involved with living with young people who are trying to find their own identity.

Those in the mid-life crisis: who are experiencing the basic limitations of human life and realize that they will not be able to achieve all their goals.

Older couples: whose children are grown and have gone out on their own and who now have to make adjustments to a new kind of life together without the constant presence of others.

Widows and widowers: who must deal with the loneliness and adjustments that result from the death of a spouse.

Retired persons: who need to find other ways of expressing themselves after leaving their jobs and professions.

The aged: who experience the often neglected and patronizing attitude of society as well as the anxiety regarding death and the pressures of living on fixed incomes and possibly being confined to a nursing home.

Single parents: who must face the responsibilities of bringing up children without the support of a spouse.

Separated and divorced persons: who have gone through the hurt of broken relationships and often face negative attitudes and responses from others in their attempts to rebuild their lives.

Members of ethnic and minority groups: who often experience the injustices resulting from prejudice and narrow-mindedness.

Those of different economic levels: who are sometimes alienated by those above or below on the economic strata.

Handicapped persons: the deaf and the mentally and physically handicapped who have special need for assistance and support.

All of these may be present in your worshiping community. They all have special educational needs to which the Christian community has a responsibility to respond. And these are just those who are present at worship.

There are many others who are not present at the celebration. Some have never heard of Jesus or the Church—and they must hear about them before they can respond.

Others are not present because they long ago rejected the Church and do not realize that the Church has changed. The reason for their rejection may no longer exist.

Others are not present because the Church has changed and they do not like the "new" Church.

The community has a responsibility to try to reach out to all these people and help them. That's why the Church needs a knowledgeable and active adult faith community to carry out its mission. The task appears staggering, and it is impossible for one or a few to accomplish it by themselves. The whole community needs to be involved to share their gifts, but there must be a group (or committee or team—see Chapter 9) to stimulate the community to be aware of its responsibilities and to strive through orderly and effective ways to fulfill them.

The Church cannot fulfill its mission unless it is striving to grow continually as an adult faith community.

Some Questions To Consider

    A. Are there any important qualities that you associate with the meaning of "adult" that are omitted in this chapter?

    B. What quality presented in this chapter does not fit with your definition of "adult"?

    C. What group(s) of adults mentioned in this chapter should be receiving the most attention and service in your local community?

Additional Resources

Young Adult Ministry Resources, Department of Education, U.S. Catholic Conference, 1312 Massachusetts Ave., N.W., Washington, D.C. 20005, 1977. (Paper, 8½ x 11, 91 pp.) This is an excellent resource for understanding the needs of young adults. It provides suggestions for planning as well as descriptions of some programs for young adults from several areas of the country.

Ministry with Young Adults in the Local Church, Lander L. Beal, Board of Discipleship, The United Methodist Church, P.O. Box 849, Nashville, Tenn. 37202, 1973. (Paper, 54 pp.) This is a concise and practical book with concrete suggestions for developing and evaluating ministry to young adults.

Ministry with Single Adults, Robert Arthur Dow, Judson Press, Valley Forge, Pa. 19481, 1977. (Paper, 175 pp.) The first three chapters on issues of young adult ministry, developing a life-style and the spontaneous person are rather good. Chapters 8-14 on ministry and suggestions for programming for single adults from age eighteen through seniors are also quite good. The middle chapters on deviant behavior do not appear necessary and may even serve to give a somewhat negative impression of singles.

The Church and the Older Person, Robert M. Gray and David O. Moberg, Wm. B. Erdmans Publishing Company, 255 Jefferson Ave., S.E., Grand Rapids, Mich. 49503, 1977. (Paper, 227 pp.) This book provides a comprehensive view of the needs and concerns of older persons and how they can be ministered to as well as minister to others.

In Wisdom and the Spirit, Sara and Richard Reichert, Paulist Press, 545 Island Road, Ramsey, N.J. 07446,

1976. (Paper, 87 pp.) This book provides a comprehensive process for a pastoral program for older persons. It includes an overview, specific units on aging, the priesthood of the elderly, prayer, reconciliation and Eucharist, and death, dying and resurrection. Craft projects are also included.

Aging Together: A Manual for Ministry with Older Adults, Social Concerns Office, Green Bay Catholic Diocese, 131 South Madison, Green Bay, Wis. 54301, 1977. (Loose leaf binder, 8½ x 11.) This is a comprehensive manual in identifying and responding to older adults. It suggests many ways of proceeding. Although much of the information provided is specific to the Wisconsin area, it is a most helpful resource for stimulating one's own thought as well as being a detailed format or process which can be applied to your own situation.

Filmstrips

Senior Adults—Needs and Problems, Broadman Films, Nashville, Tenn. 37234, 1977. (Code #4435-42, 12 minutes, 52 frames.) This brief filmstrip presents a series of problems faced by senior adults and illustrates a way by which senior adults themselves participate with their pastor in organizing to meet their needs. The filmstrip is a bit over-simplified, but it does help to raise the awareness of real needs and also make some positive practical suggestions for dealing with the needs of senior adults.

Ministering to ... Senior Adults, Broadman Films, Nashville, Tenn. 37234, 1975 (Code #443-526, 10 minutes, 42 frames.) This is also a somewhat simplified presentation of who senior adults are and what their needs are as well as some practical approaches in dealing with them. It serves to stimulate thinking without going into great depth on any particular issue.

4.
Stages Of
Psychological
Development

When a teenager becomes very moody and withdrawn and refuses to communicate, the following is often heard: "He's going through a stage." Or when a girl suddenly falls in love with her eleventh grade homeroom teacher at school and begins to talk about marriage, it is said: "She's just in one of the phases of adolescence, and she'll get over it." The various stages and phases of adolescence have been studied, identified and talked about very seriously and completely for many years. There is general agreement that adolescents do go through stages and need understanding and assistance in growing through these various stages. But many people seem to have the view that once a person passes through adolescence (however broadly it may be defined), he or she reaches adulthood. Adulthood has often been viewed as a very even life without the periods of ups and downs and challenges of different stages of growth that we have clearly seen in adolescence. Such an attitude is now being challenged on many sides.

If one believes that adulthood is a period without stages of growth, then there is no need to renew or deepen one's faith commitment. A person with such a view of adulthood will see on-going faith development as a luxury for those who are more deeply committed or involved in the life of the Church. They do not see on-going adult religious education as necessary for themselves because they have made their commitment once and for all.

However, there is a rapidly growing awareness that adulthood is not a state of evenness that one reaches at a certain age. Rather, there are as many, if not more, stages of adult development as there are for adolescents.

Erikson's Eight Ages

One of the foremost writers in the field of development stages is Erik Erikson who authored several books on psychological development. In his book *Childhood and Society* Erikson identifies eight stages which persons experience in their growth toward maturity. Each of these stages represents a critical period of development and a crisis which one must face and deal with in order to grow. These crises involve dealing with a fundamental issue and result in a basic attitude about life. In facing these crises, a person assumes a tendency toward one of two attitudes in each stage. Erikson's stages deserve a detailed explanation, but only brief examples can be given here. The interested reader can explore Erikson's own explanation in Chapter 7 of *Childhood and Society*.

1. *Trust versus mistrust*: The way parents respond or don't respond to the cries of their baby will help determine whether the child begins to have an attitude of "I can count on others" or "Nobody cares about me."

2. *Autonomy versus shame and doubt*: Children need to experience an environment where they can be autonomous and act on their own without always "getting into trouble." Children need to feel separate from others and be by themselves and feel comfortable about being by themselves. Ultimately the child can say: "I am secure apart from you."

3. *Initiative versus guilt*: Children need to be allowed to do things like help with the dishes or help paint the room

without being made to feel guilty about possible consequences (e.g., broken dishes or paint on the floor). They need guidance to express their initiative rather than constant prohibition. Parents need to provide acceptable ways of expressing initiative rather than saying: "What did you do that for?"

4. *Industry versus inferiority*: Children need to experience success in doing things such as modeling clay, drawing pictures, or putting on their own clothes. Parents can affirm by saying "Tell me about your picture" rather than "That doesn't look like a tree to me." If parents are over-critical, the child can begin to doubt his or her competence and will feel incapable of achieving anything.

5. *Identity versus role confusion*: The basic question in this stage is "Who am I?" There is often a tendency to lose oneself in a particular group in an effort to find out one's identity. Adopting a certain style of dress or associating with a special group (clique) is often done by teenagers in their quest for identity.

6. *Intimacy versus isolation*: In this stage a person can make a commitment to another or to a cause because he or she has a contribution to make while realizing and accepting the sacrifices or compromises which may be involved. Others fear making a commitment because they fear they might lose their identity. Some make a preliminary commitment and then pull back when they feel they are "getting too involved," whether this commitment be to a social group, organization, friendship, or romantic relationship.

7. *Generativity versus stagnation*: This stage is concerned with guiding and developing the next generation through one's own children or one's productivity or creativity in career or talents. Sharing of oneself, one's talents or one's gifts with others is necessary for growth; otherwise stagnation and regression result.

8. *Integrity versus despair*: This stage is the fruition of growth through the other seven stages. A person experiences a

31

wholeness and order about life. It involves an acceptance and comfortableness about life and a sense of accomplishment. Those who experience this integrity do not have a fear of dying. Those who do not experience this integrity feel that they are "running out of time." They don't have time to try another effort to reach integrity, and despair is the resulting attitude toward life.

These stages are not totally separate and distinct, and none is ever completely fulfilled. As a person grows, each stage continues to be further developed. For example, the crisis of identity versus role confusion is usually experienced intensely during adolescence, but the search for and development of one's identity continues throughout life.

Erikson points out that if a person's development in a certain stage is frustrated, it is possible for that person to remain fixated at that particular stage.

Though stated briefly here, Erikson indicates very clearly that a person's development through these stages and crises is a gradual and complicated process.

Bernard Boelen's Developmental Theory

Another author, though not as well known in this field, is Dr. Bernard Boelen of DePaul University of Chicago. This author was privileged to be a student of Boelen's at Loyola University in Chicago. Boelen has been working on a book which will be published in the near future, but until then the reader will have to rely on this author's summary of his own notes to describe the elementary points of Boelen's theory.

Boelen says that a person's growth toward maturity is a progression through the three fundamental levels of human nature: (1) the physical or biological level which makes up a person's physical structure, such as bones, skin, muscles, etc.; (2) the logical or technical level which represents a person's powers to think rationally and logically (e.g., two plus two makes four); (3) the personal or spiritual level which represents a person's powers to love another and to believe in another and to make commitments to others which go beyond logic. The personal level does not violate logic or rational thinking. Rather, it supersedes it, going beyond logic and rational thinking.

Boelen describes human development in terms of breaking through from one level to another or integrating more deeply on a particular level. He describes several early stages, but for reasons of brevity, just the later stages will be presented here. All ages mentioned are merely averages and should not be applied strictly.

Negative Stage (13-14 for women; 14-16 for men)

At this stage a person is caught between the logical level and the personal level. The person realizes that logic has limitations (e.g., how can you logically explain why a Dr. Tom Dooley would leave a lucrative medical career in this country to work among the poor in the jungles of Southeast Asia?) but has not broken through into the level of personal relationships of faith and love. This is usually a very tense and difficult period for most people. During this time teenagers often reject family, Church, and society, which is an outward expression of their negative feelings.

Early Adolescence (14-20 for women; 16-21 for men)

A person breaks through into the personal level and experiences life as an exhilarating challenge. A person develops intimate friendships and begins to appreciate the opposite sex. The world is seen as open, beautiful, and romantic. There is a tendency toward hasty and idealistic judgments. This is only the beginning of adulthood. A person can now begin to understand the meaning of faith and love even if he or she is not yet able to respond fully to these commitments. Often during this period, young persons fall in love or want to commit themselves to idealistic causes.

33

Late Adolescence (21-25 for women; 22-30 for men)

This is a period of integration and putting things together for oneself. Life-style decisions are made and careers are begun. People marry, enter religious life, or choose to be single. They make and begin to live out fundamental decisions which significantly influence the rest of their lives. During the later part of this period, a person begins to experience the tensions that arise by trying to live one's ideals and finding this difficult in the humdrum of daily existence. One often feels compelled to choose between ideals or pragmatic approaches to life.

Young Adulthood (25-30 for women; 30-40 for men)

Young adulthood is a period of further integration and consolidation. One's career is established, the family grows, and on-going friendships develop. However, there is a shift in emphasis—what was once an adventure becomes a chore or duty. People find themselves being determined by their tasks in life while the opposite was true in earlier stages. Feelings of inadequacy and limitation begin to arise. The coming generation is seen more and more as a threat because they have more energy, are better educated, and propose new and challenging ideas. People feel that "there is just not enough time." People frequently have serious doubts about previous decisions they have made. This brings a person to the threshold of maturity.

Crisis of Limits (30-40 for women; 40-45 for men)

There is a general feeling of "Is that all there is to life?" For many, life is just a series of boring activities. A person realizes that he or she will not reach all career goals. The family will not achieve all one had hoped for as a family. The body begins to deteriorate more rapidly and one is aware that there are fundamental limitations to what can be accomplished.

Some people seek to avoid this crisis by escaping in activities which take up most of their time. These activities could be hobbies, sports, drinking or loose living. Some suddenly leave family, spouse and career to seek fulfillment else-where. Whatever the activity, the general feeling is one of depression. Boelen suggests that the mature way of facing this crisis is to realize one's limitations, slow down, and try to enjoy the more meaningful things in life. Boelen also sees this period as the most critical faith crisis. For many, religion has no meaning at this time. At this time in life, a person has to face up to whether one really wants to believe and live out those beliefs. Some leave the Church, and even though some remain, their life of faith is superficial and boring. By facing this crisis and accepting our limitations, it is possible to take the time that is needed to do the valuable things in life. One can really become aware of his or her relationships with God and with others and try to make them even more meaningful.

These stages of adulthood as described by Dr. Boelen seemed to make sense to close observers of human behavior, but there was no scientific evidence available to substantiate the observations made here. However, in the last few years, there has been much more work done on studying adults and the possible growth cycles they go through.

Roger Gould's Research

One person who has done considerable research in the area of adult life stages is Dr. Roger Gould of UCLA. Gould had done several studies based on interviews with adults in which they are asked to respond to, and put in order of priority, a series of statements and questions such as: "I would be quite content to remain as old as I am now"; "For me, marriage has been a good thing"; "There's still plenty of time to do most of the things I want to do." The entire list of questions and a report on the research of Dr. Gould can be found in the February, 1975 issue of *Psychology Today*. In his work Gould has identified many different stages which adults pass through, and these stages will be described only briefly here.

Ages 16-17: Individuals in this stage want to escape from parental dominance, but they also experience concealed feelings of anxiety which result from their previous dependence on their family and the uncertainty of preparing for the future. This future seems distant and unknown. Teenagers desire to move out into their own apartment or go away to school, but they are anxious about being on their own.

Ages 18-22: In this stage people begin to substitute friends for family as they grow more independent of the family. They are more open to new and different ideas. At this time, people do move away from their families and seek their own style of life.

Ages 23-28: Those in this stage feel that they are the "now generation" and now is the time to be alive and build their future—both personally and professionally. Careers are started and many marry. Their energies are concentrated on becoming competent in the real world and they develop more self-reliance while tending to make less use of friends as a substitute for the family. Toward the later part of this period there is a decreasing feeling that "marriage has been good for me."

Ages 29-34: In the early years of this period, individuals begin to question what they are doing and why they are doing it. They discover deep strivings that were put aside during the twenties when building a workable life structure was the most important task. There is a continuing expansion of the personality, but it happens in a more leisurely fashion. There is a clear focus on the family, and special importance is given to children who are viewed as an extension of oneself. An active social life seems less important. There is a decline in the feeling that "I am content to remain as old as I am now." There is an increasing tendency to feel that parents are the cause of many unsolved stubborn personality problems. During this time parents often try to achieve through their children what they did

36

not achieve themselves, so they push children into socializing, athletics, academics and other areas of life.

Ages 35-43: At this stage, the feeling of leisurely development changes to a sense of quiet urgency. Time, once shrugged off as infinite, is now visibly finite. There is a growing feeling that "it's too late to make any changes in my career," along with a growing feeling that "I don't make enough money to do what I want." The person feels: "My personality is pretty well set." This is generally an unstable and uncomfortable period: personal comfort decreases and marital comfort remains low. During this time many change careers, leave family and spouse, or withdraw into themselves through hobbies, turn to drinking, or seek to associate with a younger generation.

Ages 44-50: During this time people begin to come to terms with time and with themselves as stable personalities. They realize that "the die is cast"; what is done is done. Money becomes less important. Life settles down and becomes more even—not better or worse, just even. Children, previously seen as extensions of oneself, are now respected as individuals as they become young adults. Friends and loved ones become more important. Marriage often becomes more meaningful and people seek deeper relationships with family and friends.

Ages 50 and over: In this period, there is a mellowing of feelings and relationships. Children are a satisfaction and parents are no longer seen as the cause of one's personality problems. Rather than on the future, the focus turns to what has been accomplished in the half-century. People are not rushed by the sense of urgency that accompanied the achieving thirties. They are more eager to have human experiences such as sharing joys, sorrows, confusions and triumphs of everyday life. Concerns about health rise, death becomes a new presence, and there is a growing feeling that "I can't do things as well as I used to do." Realizing this, many initiate

37

second careers or find fulfillment in creative hobbies.

Dr. Gould is continuing his studies, and the descriptions given here are tentative. He has reached some general conclusions. He says that the sequence of stages is generally true for most people, but the precise ages will depend on the individual's personality. The important point is to face these stages with thoughtful concentration to try to come to new beliefs about oneself and the world. In his book *Transformations* he gives a very detailed explanation of his findings. Also, a popular summary of the work of Gould and other researchers appears in the book *Passages* by Gail Sheehy.

Though there are some differences in the ages mentioned, the observations of Erikson, Boelen and Gould complement and reinforce one another. All these authors admit that their descriptions are tentative explanations and final conclusions must await further research.

While realizing that the descriptions of adult development are general and tentative, they are helpful in understanding the needs and tensions which adults experience. Effective programs for adults can be of great assistance in helping adults identify and understand these stages. Also, adults need help in facing the various crises described above in order to move through them in a growthful way. And these stages of adult development have serious implications for a person's faith. Because adults do experience these various stages and crises, one's faith commitment must be continually renewed and deepened. The various stages of faith development will be discussed in the next chapter.

It is especially important that all who hold leadership positions in the Church be thoroughly familiar with the stages of adult development in order to foster their own personal growth and then enable the growth of others.

Priests, directors of religious education, principals, committee members and other adult leaders must examine the implications of the theories of adult development for themselves first so that they can influence positively the growth of others.

Some Questions To Consider

A. What stage of development do you feel you are in right now? What are the reasons for saying you are in this stage?

B. How can the Church/parish minister to adults in enabling them to grow through these stages?

C. What particular needs or persons should be receiving significant attention in your local situation right now?

Additional Resources

Books

Childhood and Society, Erik Erikson, W. W. Norton and Co. Inc., 500 Fifth Ave., New York, N.Y. 10003, second edition, revised and enlarged, 1963. (Paper, 445 pp.) Chapter 7, "Eight Ages of Man," provides a detailed explanation of Erikson's stages of development.

Transformations—Growth and Change in Adult Life, Roger Gould, Simon and Shuster, 1230 Avenue of the Americas, New York, N.Y. 10020, 1978, (Cloth, 343 pp.) This book presents a detailed explanation of Gould's research as well as many specific examples of persons who experienced the various stages.

Passages—Predictable Crises of Adult Life, Gail Sheehy, Bantam Books, Inc., 666 Fifth Ave., New York, N.Y. 10019, 1976. (Paper, 580 pp.) While this book is rather negative regarding the influence of religion on a person's growth and makes no mention of how helpful religious groups or institutions can be, it does provide a good summary of much of the recent research on adult development. The book is easy, interesting reading. However, most of the case studies seem negative in that the people growing through stages seem to get a divorce or reject a previous life-style in the process. It is possible to grow through these stages without doing either.

A Journey to Self Through Dialogue, Thomas Downs, Twenty-Third Publications, P.O. Box 180, West Mystic, Conn. 06388, 1977. (Paper, 144 pp.) This book provides a practical and effective method for persons to understand their personal psychological and faith journeys. It is based solidly on good theology and psychology and is an excellent example of how to use the principles of andragogy—self-directed learning.

Articles

"Adult Life Stages, Growth Toward Self-Tolerance," Roger Gould, *Psychology Today*, February, 1975, pp. 74-78. Gould describes his research using graphs to show how different concerns arise at different ages.

"The Quiet Journey: Psychological Development and Religious Growth from Ages Thirty to Sixty," Henry Simmons, *Religious Education*, Vol. LXXI, No. 2, March-April 1976, pp. 132-142. Father Simmons describes the religious attitudes expressed as people age from thirty to sixty.

Cassette Tape

Mid-Life Crisis of Limits, Brother James Zullo, F.S.C., N.C.R. Cassettes, P.O. Box 281, Kansas City, Mo. 64141, 1977. (National Catholic Reporter Publishing Co., 4 cassettes, 3 hours.) These lectures discuss the physical and emotional changes of the mid-life years and suggest steps for dealing with the tensions and issues that arise. Brother Zullo proposes a spirituality for mid-life using the letters of St. Paul as a rich resource.

5.
Faith And
Moral Development

The preceding chapter on psychological development poses several implications for growth in faith. If a person makes a faith commitment at one stage of development, the commitment will have to be renewed or deepened at a later stage. Faith commitments that are not renewed will gradually fade and die.

Since the stages of psychological growth have implications for a faith growth, the whole area of growth in faith is now being seriously reconsidered. Earlier writers such as St. John of the Cross and St. Teresa of Avila described stages of growth in the spiritual life. These works are being re-examined today to see what light they can provide for understanding growth in faith.

At the present time John Westerhoff III and James W. Fowler are prominent authors in the field of faith development. Lawrence Kohlberg is the most noted author on moral development. The work of these three will be described briefly here.

John Westerhoff—Styles of Faith

In Chapter 4 of his book *Will Our Children Have Faith?* John Westerhoff identifies four "styles" of faith. He uses the analogy of a tree to describe faith growth. A tree with three years of growth (therefore, three rings) is just as much a complete and whole tree as a tree with six rings. The same is true of faith. Each style of faith is complete and whole, and one style is not better than another.

A tree grows if it has the proper environment and nourishment—sunlight, water and minerals. Likewise, we expand in faith when we have a proper environment—interactions and relations with other believing persons.

Just as a tree grows slowly, adding one ring at a time, without skipping rings, so, too, we expand in faith slowly and gradually over a period of time.

As the tree grows, it does not eliminate earlier rings, but adds on new rings. So we, too, do not grow out of one style of faith and into another. Rather, we expand into each new style of faith while retaining the needs of all the earlier styles. In fact, Westerhoff points out that if the needs of an earlier style cease to be met, the person has a tendency to return to that earlier style. Expansion in faith will not continue until the needs of the earlier styles are reasonably satisfied.

Keeping the aspects of the tree-faith analogy in mind, consider Westerhoff's description of the four styles of faith.

Experienced Faith: During the early childhood years, children act with experienced faith. They imitate and respond to the actions of others. Being hugged and caressed is a fundamental need of this style. The language used to transmit faith must accompany concrete experiences. Words such as trust, love and acceptance will be empty without experiences of trust, love and acceptance. In this style, faith is experienced enactively—through interactions with other believers. The faith of children is really the faith of their parents and other adults because the children imitate and respond to the actions of these adults.

Not only children live by experienced faith. Adults have

these same needs—even if our culture seems to try to repress them.

Affiliative Faith: A person with affiliative faith needs to feel that he or she belongs to a *community* and that one is important to that community and its activities. Another characteristic of affiliative faith is the importance of religious *affections*. This is very much a "religion of the heart" and a person needs to experience awe, wonder and mystery. Moreover a person with affiliative faith needs a strong *sense of authority* in the community's affirmation of a story that judges and inspires its actions. Learning the community's *story* is essential for faith.

For junior high students it is especially important to provide a group which has lots of activities where they can be actively involved.

Searching Faith: This style is quite different from the previous one. *Doubt* and/or *critical judgment* are necessary for a person in this style. People in searching faith need to set themselves against the community's story to test it. During this time, "religion of the head" becomes as equally important as "religion of the heart."

Also, a person with searching faith goes through a period of *experimentation* in which other traditions and stories are investigated. And the third characteristic of searching faith is the need to *commit one's life* to persons and causes—if only for a short period of time. This often seems fickle, but it is the way that people learn to make commitments and achieve convictions which are truly one's own. Teenagers frequently question the Church and seek out other churches or get involved in specific movements in their search for faith. Youth retreats are an effective way to listen to and respond to their questions.

Owned Faith: Owned faith is the culmination of the process called *conversion*—the movement from experienced and affiliative faith through searching faith to a personal commitment to a life-style where one's words are expressed in actions. Persons with owned faith give witness to that faith in word and deed and they struggle to eliminate the discrepancy between what they say they believe and what they actually do. People in this style frequently become involved in prayer groups and efforts to serve the poor and handicapped in an intense way.

Westerhoff says that owned faith is God's intention for everyone, and that we are all called to reach our fullest potential. However, Jesus lived and died and rose for all persons, and all are within God's grace, no matter what style of faith they have.

Westerhoff suggests that the Church has not encouraged people to challenge and question the story, so many people have *not* expanded through searching faith into owned faith. It is also this author's experience that many Catholic adults have never experienced a time of questioning and therefore are very uncomfortable when others question the Church. Some leave the Church because "there aren't any answers anymore."

James Fowler—Stages in Faith

John Westerhoff acknowledges that his work on faith development was greatly stimulated by the research and writing of James Fowler. Fowler has identified six stages of faith development. He describes his research and his descriptions of the stages in Chapter 7 of *Values and Moral Development*, edited by Thomas C. Hennessy, S.J. He admits that his conclusions are tentative and that much more research must be done. A brief description of Fowler's six stages follows:

Stage One—Intuitive-Projective Faith: The child's world is intuitive and filled with fantasy, and the child is strongly and permanently influenced by the examples, feelings, language and actions of important adults, such as parents. Children, for good or ill, often imitate the actions of their parents in church.

Stage Two—Mythical-Literal Faith: A person takes for himself or herself the stories, beliefs and observances that are part of belonging to one's community. Attitudes are observed and adopted and literal interpretation of beliefs and moral rules are assumed. Symbols are one-dimensional and literal. Authority (especially parental) has more influence than peers. More than once parents have been confronted with the statement, "But Father Smith said we should do it this way."

Stage Three—Synthetic-Conventional Faith: The person's world extends beyond family and primary social groups into school, work, peers, friendships, etc. Faith must provide a meaningful synthesis of these now more complex involvements. Meaning is authenticated by either a properly designated authority in each sphere or by a consensus of "those who count." Persons in this stage are greatly influenced by peers. A junior high student may be very involved or not involved in a parish youth group—depending on whether his or her friends are involved or not.

Stage Four—Individuating-Reflexive Faith: Here the person (usually in late adolescence) must begin to take seriously the burden of taking responsibility for his or her commitments, life-style, beliefs and attitudes. In this stage a person must face the tensions between: being an individual and belonging to a community; subjectivity and objectivity; self-fulfillment and service to others; relative and absolute. A person in stage four often finds it necessary to resolve these tensions by choosing one pole or the other. For a person in stage four, the ability to decide often means that one set of values or commitments is over-emphasized to the neglect of the alternatives. Teenagers frequently choose an extreme position for or against the Church because they are in this stage. Some adults in this stage reject any others who do not hold the same opinion as theirs.

Stage Five—Paradoxical-Consolidative Faith: Stage Five is an advance in that a person recognizes the integrity and truth in positions of others. A person can affirm and live out his or her own commitments while honoring that which is true in the lives of others. In stage five a person is ready for community beyond class or ideological distinctions and knows the cost and is willing to pay the cost of being part of a community. Values are espoused and risk and action are part of one's life. Persons in this stage can accept differences of opinion among people in their faith community, and they seriously try to live out their convictions.

Stage Six—Universalizing Faith: This stage of faith is rare. What Christians and Jesus called the kingdom of God is a lived, felt reality in a person's life. One dwells *in* the world as a transforming presence, but is not *of* the world. The sense of oneness of all living persons is a permeating reality and a basis for decision and action. A person's participation in the Ultimate is immediate and direct. Such a person is ready for fellowship with anyone at any other stage and any other faith tradition. Fowler has indicated in conversation with this author that he knows of very few people in this stage. He pointed out Mother Teresa of Calcutta as one such person.

If Fowler and Westerhoff are on target, their differing yet similar descriptions of faith development seriously question any understanding of faith as a static existence which one either has or doesn't have. Faith is a dynamic, growing or regressing experience. A person can always grow in faith.

These descriptions of faith development can provide light for understanding some of the phenomena seen in the Church today. For example, there is a strong effort in many areas to return to previous methods and tools of instruction such as the Baltimore Catechism. There are the Tridentine Mass groups and others who want to return to Latin. There is much oppositon to the involvement of Church leaders in social justice issues. The question arises: "What's happening to the Church?"

As mentioned earlier, Westerhoff says that few adults

were encouraged to challenge and test the community's story, so few expanded through searching faith into owned faith. Moreover, the Roman Catholic story has experienced many changes in the last twenty years. If the question "What does it mean to be a Catholic?" were asked twenty years ago, typical answers might well have been: "Mass on Sunday, in Latin," "No meat on Friday," "Fast and abstinence during Lent," "Baltimore Catechism," etc. Now many of these responses are no longer given. If you were to ask Catholics today "What does it mean to be Catholic?" the responses would be very different. Thus, many Catholics feel that their "old story" is now changed into a "new story" which they are not comfortable with. Since most have not expanded into owned faith, they have not achieved a story they can call "my story." Thus, many needs of affiliative faith (being part of a community that has a story and a clear sense of authority) are no longer being met. So people are reaching back to the "old story" to meet those needs. These people are in affiliative faith. This is an authentic style of faith, but they should be offered the opportunity to expand in faith or at least to understand that there are other authentic styles of faith.

Much more needs to be done in order to understand more fully how faith develops. And much more needs to be done to help people expand and grow in faith so that they can realize that the *real story* of what it means to be a Catholic today is an evolving story with a varied and complicated tradition and even more diverse future because the Spirit is continually at work in the community of believers and the world.

Lawrence Kohlberg—Moral Development

Related to faith is the area of life involving moral decision making. For over twenty years the prominent name in the study of moral development has been Lawrence Kohlberg. He has done both longitudinal and cross-cultural studies on the reasoning used in making moral judgments. His work is described in Chapter II of *Moral Development: A Guide to Piaget and Kohlberg* by Ronald Duska and Mariellen Whelan. Kohlberg has identified six stages with two stages occurring within three distinct levels. The levels and stages are briefly described here:

Level I: Pre-Conventional: At this level a child responds to rules and labels of good and bad, right and wrong, but these labels are interpreted in terms of physical or pleasurable consequences of the actions or in terms of the physical power of those who make up the labels and rules.

Stage 1: Obedience-Punishment Orientation: A child makes decisions in order to avoid punishment. An act is considered good or bad according to the physical consequences of the action. A person's behavior is determined by giving in to superior power. Typical reasoning on this level might be: "I won't do it because I'll be punished," or "It's okay because I won't get caught."

Stage 2: Personal Interest Orientation: In this slightly more developed stage, a person considers an action to be "right" if it satisfies one's personal needs and sometimes the needs of others. The attitude is one of "What will I get out of it?" A sense of fairness begins to develop in that a person will do something for another *if* that other will do something in return. It's an "I'll scratch your back if you scratch mine" situation. The person is concerned about getting his or her share. Children often say, "I'll give you a piece of candy if you let me play with your toy."

Level II: Conventional: On this level the person is concerned about keeping rules and conforming to what the family, group or nation expects. Maintaining the established order and identifying with the persons or group involved in it are important.

Stage 3: Good Boy or Good Girl Orientation: At this stage a person is concerned with pleasing others and being approved by them. An individual will make decisions in order to gain approval from the important persons in his or her life (parents, spouse, friends, peer group). A child may disobey a parent in order to win approval from the peer group. "But Mom, all the other kids were doing it!"

Stage 4: Law and Order Orientation: Here a person is concerned about authority, fixed rules and maintaining the present social order. Right behavior consists of fulfilling one's obligations and promoting the established system. Some people defended the existence of discriminatory practices against blacks because it was the law at the time.

Level III: Post-Conventional: At this level, there is a clear effort to define moral values and principles which have validity in themselves apart from the people or groups who hold these principles even at the risk of not being accepted by the group.

Stage 5: Greater Good of Society Orientation: Right action tends to be defined in terms of individual rights and standards which have been examined and accepted by the whole society. Realizing the relativism of personal values, there is an emphasis on consensus. There is an awareness of need for laws and rules, but rules can be changed for the greater good of society. This is basically majority rule but not in a rigid or frozen sense as in stage 4. Outside the realm of law, free agreement and contract are the binding element of obligation. Persons in this stage who disagreed with discriminatory laws against blacks worked to have the laws changed through the legislative process.

Stage 6: Universal Ethical Principle Orientation: Right action is defined by the decision of conscience in accord with self-chosen ethical principles which are logically consistent and universal. These principles are abstract and ethical and not concrete rules like the Ten Commandments. At heart they are universal principles of justice, equality of human beings and respect for the dignity of human beings as individual persons.

51

Because discriminatory laws against blacks violated basic human rights, persons in this stage participated in activities of civil disobedience such as sit-ins and refused to sit in the back of buses.

In his studies Kohlberg has found that the majority of the adults in the United States do *not* progress beyond stage 4. He also points out that the U.S. Constitution is basically a stage 5 document. Thus, it is quite possible that many adults in the U.S. would ordinarily not operate at a moral judgment level that is consistent with the founding principles of our country.

These descriptions of faith and moral development are presented briefly in order to stimulate those using this booklet to reflect on the necessity for helping adults grow. Many adults still operate on the assumption that adulthood is a plateau reached at the age of twenty-one. The overwhelming evidence shows that adulthood is an ever-developing process—even in the areas of faith and moral decision making. Helping people to understand this and to continue growing is an important responsibility of those involved in adult religious education.

Some Questions To Consider

A. What stage(s) of faith and moral development do you feel you are in?

B. What phenomena in your local situation can be clarified and understood through these descriptions of faith and moral development?

C. How can the Church/parish minister to adults to enable them to grow in their understanding and living of faith?

Additional Resources

The Church as Reflecting Community: Models of Adult Religious Learning, Loretta Girzaitis, Twenty-Third

Publications, P.O. Box 180, West Mystic, Conn. 06388, 1977. (Paper, 8½ x 11, 186 pp.) Chapter 7 is very helpful in describing faith development concisely and suggesting programs to encourage it.

Will Our Children Have Faith? John H. Westerhoff III, The Seabury Press, 815 Second Avenue, New York, N.Y. 10017, 1976. (Cloth, 126 pp.) This excellent little book provides the description of Westerhoff's styles of faith (Chapter 4) as well as his suggestions for applications in the future.

"Faith Development Theory and the Aims of Religious Education," James W. Fowler, pages 187-208 in *Emerging Issues In Religious Education*, ed. by Gloria Durka and Joanmarie Smith, Paulist Press, 545 Island Road, Ramsey, N.J. 07446, 1976. (Paper, 211 pp.) This article provides a description of Fowler's research and his stages of faith.

Moral Development: A Guide to Piaget and Kohlberg, Ronald Duska and Mariellen Whelan, Paulist Press, 545 Island Road, Ramsey, N.J. 07446, 1975. (Paper, 128 pp.) This small book provides a good understanding of Kohlberg's research and conclusions as well as specific suggestions for application.

"Stages in Faith: The Structural-Developmental Approach," James W. Fowler, pages 173-211 in *Values and Moral Development*, ed. by Thomas C. Hennessy, S.J., Paulist Press, 545 Island Road, Ramsey, N.J. 07446, 1976. (Paper, 234 pp.) This article is somewhat more comprehensive than the preceding reference on Fowler and provides essentially the same description of the research and stages of faith.

Understanding Stages of Moral Development: A Programmed Learning Workbook, Susan Pagliuso, Paulist Press, 545 Island Road, Ramsey, N.J. 07446, 1976. (Paper, 8½ x 11, 151 pp.) This book enables the reader to experience the actual thinking processes Kohlberg describes.

"What Does Fowler Have To Say to Adult Educators?" Stephen C. Gilmour, *The Living Light*, Vol. 13, No. 4, Winter 1976, pages 524-535. This article describes Fowler's theory and discusses the implications for adult education.

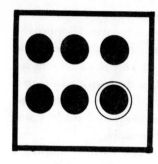

6.
What Is
Andragogy?

The word "pedagogy" is familiar to many people as being related to the education of children. In recent decades much research has been devoted to educational approaches and techniques that are most appropriate for adults. Dr. Malcolm Knowles, now at North Carolina State University, is one of the foremost names in the field of adult education. In his book *The Modern Practice of Adult Education* he has given a comprehensive description of his developing theory and convictions about the methods that are most appropriate for adult learning. Dr. Knowles has popularized the term "andragogy" to refer to those methods that are best suited to adult learning. The word is coined from the two Greek words "aner" (with the stem "andr-") which means "man" (the Greeks had no word for an adult "woman") and "agogus" meaning "leading." Andragogy is then defined as "the art and science of helping adults learn." This is parallel to the meaning of pedagogy—the art and science of teaching children—which comes from the Greek stem "paid" (meaning "child") and "agogus" (leading).

There has been much discussion over the issue of whether andragogy really is different from the approaches being taken in progressive education today. Leon McKenzie has addressed this issue directly in the Summer 1977 issue of *Adult Education* with an article entitled "The Issue of Andragogy." Whether or not one accepts andragogy as a distinct educational approach will depend, says McKenzie, on whether one takes a classical or phenomenological view of education. This issue may never be finally resolved, but it is important to deal with adults in a manner appropriate to them. Therefore, the basic assumptions of andragogy will be briefly described here, and readers will have to begin to resolve the issue for themselves.

Malcolm Knowles has described several basic assumptions regarding the differences between teacher-directed learning (which has characterized much of education for children) and self-directed learning (which is foundational to adult learning). Knowles suggests the following areas for examining these assumptions:

1. *The concept of the learner*: In teacher-directed learning, the learner is seen as a dependent personality who must be directed by others in making decisions and fulfilling needs. In self-directed learning, the learner is seen as an increasingly self-directed personality who can make decisions on his or her own and determine his or her own needs.

2. *Experience*: In teacher-directed learning, the experience of the learner is viewed as limited, or as something to build on, rather than as a resource for learning. In self-directed learning the experience of the learner is viewed as a rich resource for learning which can be shared with others as a part of the learning experience.

3. *Readiness to learn*: With teacher-directed learning, the learning usually varies with the physical maturity and mental development of the learner. The term "developmental task" has been used to describe the specific learning that is needed at a particular moment or period. In self-directed learning, readiness for learning usually develops out of one's specific problems or tasks in life.

4. *Orientation to learning*: In teacher-directed learning, the orientation to learning is usually toward specific subjects

which are presented in a logical development. In self-directed learning, the orientation to learning is usually toward specific problems one faces or tasks one has to accomplish.

5. *Motivation*: With teacher-directed learning, motivation is usually developed through external rewards or punishments (often associated with grades or promotion), while, with self-directed learning, motivation usually arises from internal incentives such as curiosity or the desire to solve a problem or accomplish a task.

6. *Time perspective*: Teacher-directed learning often involves postponed application of the learning (learn algebra I now so that you can learn calculus later so you can teach mathematics) while self-directed learning usually involves immediate application of what has been learned.

Malcolm Knowles is careful to point out that these differences should not be viewed as black/white distinctions. Rather they should be seen as the poles of continuum, and all good educational processes should try to enable persons to be more self-directed in their learning.

Knowles goes on to describe the difference in processes used in teacher-directed and self-directed learning. The process elements he addresses are: the learning climate, planning, needs diagnosis, goal-setting, designing a learning plan, learning activities, and evaluation. A concise overview of the comparison of the assumptions and processes of teacher-directed and self-directed learning is given in the chart at the end of this chapter.

A serious consideration of one's assumptions regarding learning is necessary for anyone involved in adult religious education, for it is very important to deal with adults as adults in a manner that is appropriate to their needs and style of learning.

Some Questions To Consider

A. Is andragogy really a specific approach to learning or

is it just another name for the best developments of pedagogy?

B. What assumptions do you personally make about the adults you deal with in your local adult education situation?

C. What specific aspects of andragogy are presently missing or weakly applied in your local efforts to provide adult religious education opportunities?

Additional Resources

The Modern Practice of Adult Education—Andragogy Versus Pedagogy, Malcolm S. Knowles, Association Press, 291 Broadway, New York, N.Y. 10007. (Cloth, 384 pp.) This is perhaps the most comprehensive book on adult education now in print. The author gives theory and principles as well as practical guidance in assessing needs, translating objectives into program designs, and evaluation. Chapter 3 is especially helpful in understanding the elements of andragogy.

Adult Religious Education: The 20th-Century Challenge, Leon McKenzie, Twenty-Third Publications, P.O. Box 180, West Mystic, Conn. 06388, 1975. (Paper, 160 pp.) Chapter 4 describes andragogy and addresses the arguments for and against considering it to be a specific approach to adult learning.

"The Issues of Andragogy," Leon McKenzie, *Adult Education: A Journal of Research and Theory*, Volume XXVII, Number 4, Summer 1977, pages 225-229. McKenzie discusses the different views regarding andragogy about whether it is simply a new word or really a new theory for adult education.

A Trainers Guide to Andragogy, John D. Ingalls, U.S. Department of Health, Education and Welfare, revised edition, 1973. (Paper, 242 pp.) Purchase from U.S. Government Printing Office, Washington, D.C. 20402. Stock #017-061-00033-0, Catalog #HE 17.8:AN2/973. This book was commissioned by HEW to apply the principles of andragogy to the social service areas. It gives the basic principles and then suggests several sample workshops which can be easily adapted to adult education situations—particularly for training leaders in adult education.

A COMPARISON OF THE *ASSUMPTIONS* AND *PROCESSES* OF TEACHER-DIRECTED (PEDAGOGICAL) LEARNING AND SELF-DIRECTED (ANDRAGOGICAL) LEARNING

ASSUMPTIONS		
About	**Teacher-Directed Learning**	**Self-Directed Learning**
Concept of the learner	Dependent personality	Increasingly self-directed personality
Role of learner's experience	To be built on more than used	A rich resource for learning
Readiness to learn	Varies with levels of maturation	Develops from life tasks and problems
Orientation to learning	Subject-centered	Task- or problem-centered
Motivation	External rewards and punishments	Internal incentives curiosity
Time Perspective	Postponed application	Immediacy of application

(Please read as poles on a spectrum, not as black and white differences.) Developed by Malcolm S. Knowles, Department of Adult and Community College Education, North Carolina State University.

PROCESS ELEMENTS		
Elements	Teacher-Directed Learning	Self-Directed Learning
Climate	Formal authority-oriented Competitive Judgmental	Informal Mutually respectful Consensual Collaborative Supportive
Planning	Primarily by teacher	By participative decision-making
Diagnosis of needs	Primarily by teacher	By mutual assessment
Setting goals	Primarily by teacher	By mutual negotiation
Designing a learning plan	Content units, course syllabus, logical sequence	Learning projects Learning contracts Sequenced in terms of readiness Problem units
Learning activities	Transmittal techniques Assigned readings	Inquiry projects Independent study Experimental techniques
Evaluation	Primarily by teacher	By mutual assessment of self-collected evidence

61

7.
Motivating Adults

In gatherings of people who are responsible for planning and implementing programs for adult religious education, the topic of conversation soon turns to "How do you get them to participate?" Motivating adults to be involved in learning programs is generally considered to be one of the thorniest problems for those involved in adult religious education. Many of the well-known practitioners in adult education have addressed this problem.

The Fundamental Problem

Father Kevin Coughlin, in a paper entitled "Motivating Adults for Religious Education," prepared for the National Conference of Diocesan Directors of Religious Education—CCD, presents his conviction that the lack of motivation flows mainly from the fact that most Catholic adults do not understand that they are the *Church* and the fact that they do not feel and experience a spirit of community in the Church. Coughlin points out that there are presently existing in the Church two models for religious education.

The "old" model reaches out toward children, takes place mainly in classrooms, and focuses on doctrines. The "new" model involves adults, takes place wherever the community is present, and emphasizes a way of life. He contrasts them this way:

"old" model	*"new" model*
children	adults
classroom	community
doctrines	a way of life

Coughlin points out that the "old" model is really relatively new—it developed only during the last four hundred years. The "new" model is really quite ancient because it dates back to the earliest Christian communities and how they educated the members to live what they believed.

Coughlin stresses that the community is always educating—whether it realizes it or not, whether it wants to or not. Parents are religious educators, for good or ill, whether they want to be or not, by the mere fact that they are parents. Coughlin says that the community cannot avoid the role of educator. Its only alternatives are: (1) to be conscious of this role or not, and (2) whether to do it well or poorly. He is convinced that the basic need in motivation is to enable people to realize that they (and not just the pope, bishops and priests) are the Church and that there must be a vibrant, concerned community of adult believers if good religious education is to take place at any level.

If adults considered themselves to be vitally important to the Church and if they felt responsible for the Church, they would be greatly interested in participating in programs that would enable them to fulfill this responsibility. Many adults see themselves as belonging to the Church as to a club or organization, and they look to others—such as clergy and other full-time professionals in ministerial roles—to be the leaders. There are signs that this attitude is changing, but it is still the prevailing mood with the overwhelming number of adults.

Needs

Dr. Malcolm Knowles considers motivation in terms of responding to a person's *needs*. In Chapter 5 of *The Modern Practice of Adult Education*, Knowles discusses the following needs and their implication for adult education.

1. *Physical needs.* These are the most easily observed and consciously experienced because they involve maintaining the body. People need to be able to see, hear, be comfortable and have periodic times for rest. Programs which do not respond to these needs in their implementation will not attract participants after the first session. Chairs and rooms must be comfortable for adults if they are to give their attention to the learning experience.

2. *Growth needs.* These are concerned with the fundamental urge to keep growing as a person. There seems to be a growing awareness of this urge in many adults, and they will seek programs which help them to grow.

3. *The need for security.* This need goes beyond physical safety and also includes one's self-respect and self-image. This need often motivates people to be cautious and reserved in a strange setting. People need to be treated with respect. When this need is not satisfied or is violated, some react by withdrawing into a shell, and others try to protect themselves by dominating or controlling the situation.

4. *The need for new experience.* People do seek security but there is also present a curiosity for adventure or excitement. Because of this people are motivated to seek new friends and new ideas and experiences. Adults will not continue in programs which they perceive to be the same old thing.

5. *The need for affection.* People need to be liked. This is a basic social need—even though some use strange

65

methods to achieve it. When people feel they are not liked they respond in a great variety of ways, ranging from the extremes of pouting and withdrawing to lashing out aggressively.

6. *The need for recognition.* Every person needs to feel worthwhile and will try to satisfy this need by seeking status in some group. When this need is not being fulfilled, people will do many things, sometimes in bizarre behavior, to get attention.

Dr. Knowles points out that even though some people are not yet consciously aware of these needs, the adult educator must understand them and take them into account in planning and implementing programs. Needs arousal is often one of the first challenges an adult educator will face.

Interests

In addition to needs, Malcolm Knowles also points out that people are motivated by their *interests.* He says that a need is often expressed by a "want" or a "desire." An interest can be expressed as a "liking" or a "preference." Interests are very personal and therefore differ greatly from person to person. Using the work of Irving Perge, he groups interest under the headings of what people (1) want to *gain* (health, time, money, confidence, etc.), (2) want to *be* (good parents, influential over others, recognized, etc.), (3) want to *do* (express themselves, acquire things, improve themselves, etc.), and (4) want to *save* (work, risks, embarrassment, etc.).

Interests are influenced by many factors such as socioeconomic level, education, occupation, etc. And a person's interests change as one progresses along the life cycle. Because of the variation from person to person and the change in one person's interests over time, it is vital to do much work in determining the interests of those who are expected to participate in adult religious education programs, as well as the interests of the Church community in sponsoring programs for adults.

Social Roles and Developmental Tasks

Another way of considering motivation is in terms of enabling people to fulfill their *social roles*. In Chapter 3 of *The Modern Practice of Adult Education*, Knowles summarizes the work of Dr. Robert Havighurst who has written much on social roles and the developmental tasks one must perform to fulfill these roles. Every person has certain roles in life such as spouse, parent, friend, worker, etc. To fulfill these roles, we must perform various tasks such as selecting a mate, rearing children, managing a home, finding a job, etc. These tasks also relate to certain periods of life such as early adulthood (starting a family), middle age (adjusting to aging parents), and later maturity (adjusting to death of a spouse).

These social roles and developmental tasks involve a certain readiness to learn, a "teachable moment." Because of this, programs should be timed for these adults experiencing these "teachable moments." These developmental tasks can provide some guidance for grouping various adult learners (e.g., a program for parents should include groups for parents of young children and parents of teenagers).

Much more study has to be done on the role of "believer" and the possible developmental tasks related to this role. And while the area of social roles and developmental tasks may provide fruitful results in motivating adults to participate in adult religious education programs, it should not be the only or even the primary approach taken. A comprehensive approach is needed.

Different Kinds of Motivation

Fr. James Schaefer, former director of adult religious education for the Archdiocese of Baltimore and principal author of GIFT (Growth in Faith Together) has indentified five different kinds of motivation. He discusses these in the Fall 1974 issue of *The Living Light* in the article "Motivation for Adult Religious Education."

Motivation by obligation. Educational events are incorporated into or attached to events which adults feel obligated to attend such as programs during Lent (the "do something for Lent" idea), Sunday Mass or programs to help parents prepare their children for first reception of the sacraments. Schaefer cautions that this form of motivation should be used reluctantly. Obliging adults to participate does not usually fit well with the principle of treating adults as self-directing persons.

Motivation by attraction. This is especially needed when programs are planned without prior input from the participants (or at least some of them) and usually involves well-known speakers, curiosity-arousing titles, eye-catching brochures, bulletin announcements, posters, radio and TV spots, telephone calls, mailings, etc. Through motivation by attraction, the program designers try to "sell" the program to participants through a comprehensive publicity effort.

Motivation by contagion. This happens when one adult who has responded enthusiastically to a program invites and encourages others to participate. This personal contact usually has far greater effect than the best publicity campaign. It is also a reason why program planners need not be discouraged by small numbers in the beginning of their programs.

Motivation by responsibility. This is closely related to fulfilling one's social roles and responsibilities in life. People want to be successful in what they do—whether it be as a spouse, parent, worker, parish council member, lector or catechist. Once people accept a role, they usually seek or respond to programs they see as helpful to them. Schaefer points out that programs to help catechists be better in their work and programs to assist parents in preparing their children for the sacraments have been the most successful and best received

Catholic adult education programs in recent years. This kind of motivation by responsibility is the most appropriate approach to take in attracting parents to sacramental preparation programs.

Motivation by ignition. This means sparking the inner potential for growth that adults have, but rarely use. This is hard to do, but once it is started, it is long-lasting and satisfying. To do this, it is often necessary to help adults become aware of their continuing need for growth and the various stages of development that adults pass through (refer to Chapter 4). Schaefer mentions several self-diagnostic tools which have been developed to enable adults to discover where they are and where they would like to be. The tool used by Malcolm Knowles is described on pages 274-284 of *The Modern Practice of Adult Education.*

Fr. Schaefer used a similar self-diagnostic tool in the first phase of GIFT in the Archdiocese of Baltimore (see Chapter 11 for more information on GIFT).

What Then Do We Do To Motivate?

Much has been said *about* motivation, but is there anything that can be done in a practical way? *Yes!*

Responsibility: First of all, it is essential to realize that motivation is not just one person's or the adult education committee's responsibility. Everyone involved in leadership roles in the parish has a responsibility to motivate adults to continue growing in understanding and to live what they believe. Priests have a serious responsibility because they are visible in liturgical leadership, and their ministerial roles require that they set an example. The role of the pastor is crucial. His attitude can enliven or dampen the spirit of a parish with regard to adult religious education. Associate pastors, ministers of religious education, school principals, pastoral associates, parish council members, committee members and others all are responsible for motivating adults by working together to build vibrant and effective communities. Without such cooperation and willingness, any further efforts to motivate will have short term effects at best. Responsibility is not just something carried out through words. Parish leaders just can't *say* adult education is important—they have to show it is important to them by participating in the adult programs of the parish.

Awareness: Many adults in the Church are not aware of the reasons for and the need for their own continuing religious education. They are still operating out of the "old" model mentioned by Coughlin which dealt with children. Before being motivated to continue their learning, they need to be aware of the mission of the Church and the essential role of a believing adult community to fulfill that mission (see Chapter 2). They need to be aware of what it means to be adult in the Church (Chapter 3) and the various stages of adult psychological and faith development (Chapters 4 and 5). They need to be aware of the approaches and methods that are most appropriate for adult learners (Chapter 6). They need to be aware that to stay alive and effective the Church must continually renew itself—which means change—which means that the adult believers must continually renew themselves—and grow.

This awareness will not come about through one or two bulletin announcements or announcements from the pulpit. However, it can steadily grow when the parish leadership becomes aware of these needs and all their activities are permeated with this awareness. Homilies, bulletins, letters, programs for parents, the way youth learn about and live their religion, parish council meetings, telephone calls, liturgy planning sessions and, best of all, personal interaction with others are all ways of raising this awareness of the need for continual religious learning.

Climate: We all know that the weather influences our feelings. If it's too hot or too cold, we can't get enthused about learning. This is true for adult religious education, but climate means much more than the weather. The learning climate includes the physical room and the comfortableness of the chairs. The climate includes how people are welcomed as they enter and thanked as they leave. But, most of all, the learning climate includes the spirit of the whole parish and not just the adult education committee. Is the parish alive? Do the Sunday liturgies awaken new insights and build the spirit of community? Do people enjoy coming to worship because they feel a spirit of enthusiasm and togetherness? Are people welcomed and accepted with warmth and genuine friendship? Do those involved in parish work show to the whole parish that they believe it is good to be a member of this Christian community, or do they exhibit a doomsday spirit that everything is wrong in the Church, and it would be so nice to get back to the "good old days"? If the prevailing attitude is one that "everything is wrong" in the Church, this will catch on quickly, and there won't be much enthusiasm for continuing adult education to learn about these disturbing "new things."

The pastor and full-time parish staff members play a crucial role in setting the climate in a parish. If they are convinced that the participation of the parish community is vitally necessary in making decisions concerning the parish, and if they encourage input and welcome involvement, they will, at the same time, be building a positive spirit. In doing this, it is important for them to smile frequently, treat people with respect, deal openly with disagreements, and give honest reasons when they don't agree. When they don't know the answer to a question, they should be willing to say "I don't know."

A positive attitude and a spirit of openness and enthusiasm among staff members, parish council members and other parish leaders are crucial to building the spirit of community and thereby encouraging people to continue learning. This experience of community is the fundamental element that is missing from many situations, and if Kevin Coughlin is cor-

71

rect, it is the element that must be present if the adult community is to participate actively in adult religious education experiences.

Good Planning and Implementation: It is generally agreed that poor programs are probably the biggest factor in discouraging people from continuing their religious learning. Obviously if people are turned off by a poor program, they will be reluctant to return to the next one. It is important, then, that programs for adults be good experiences for them, so that they will be inclined to return and bring someone with them (motivation by contagion).

There is a growing awareness that the effectiveness of a program is nearly always directly proportional to the amount of planning that was done beforehand. This planning must be orderly and in tune with good principles of adult learning. Chapter 8 of this book deals with adult learning principles, and Chapter 10 suggests a planning process.

As far as possible, planning for adult religious education should be based on real needs, both individual and community, and the interests of the participants. To do this, there must be a serious effort made to determine these needs and interests. Once people are asked what their needs and interests are, they must be responded to. If they can't be responded to, an honest explanation must be given. Motivation lapses sharply when people are asked to reveal their needs and then no response is made to them.

Publicity is very important. It must be aimed at adults and done in an adult manner. It is necessary to publicize a program in as many ways as possible, and there are lots of ways other than pulpit announcements. Pulpit announcements undermine their effectiveness as well as take away from the spirit of worship when done too frequently. The best kind of publicity is personal contact.

In implementing programs it is vital to understand how adults learn and what their needs are. Since adults experience many demands on their time, it is important to start on time and end on time. It is also important that there be an opportunity for discussion and interaction. Refreshments and breaks are essential for adults.

It is very important that the program planners also be involved as participants to give witness to the conviction that adult religious education is a need for everyone and not something that "we" do for "them."

A good program that is planned and implemented according to good principles of adult learning will be one of the best attractions for encouraging people to continue and to invite others to join them.

Even after all these approaches to motivation (building community, creating a positive climate, raising awareness, sharing responsibility and planning effectively) have been attempted, motivation will remain a serious challenge. It is a factor that can always be improved. Realizing this, planners should not become complacent or discouraged about the lack of motivation for continued religious learning. The important issue is to see that sure strides are made, even if they are slow, toward increasing the awareness of all adults in the community about the need for continued learning in order to understand and live their faith more fully.

Some Questions To Consider

    A. What is your reaction to Kevin Coughlin's suggestion that the most significant obstacle to motivating adults is the lack of a vibrant experience of community?

    B. How would you describe the "climate" of your local parish community? Does it enhance or lessen a person's interest in adult religious education.?

    C. What efforts have you already attempted to improve the motivation of adults regarding participation in programs of adult religious education? How successful were they?

Additional Resources

The Modern Practice of Adult Education—Andragogy Versus Pedagogy, Malcolm S. Knowles, Association Press, 291 Broadway, New York, N.Y. 10007, 1970. (Cloth, 384 pp.) Chapter 5 presents a comprehensive approach to understanding needs and interests and many suggestions for assessing them. Pages 41-48 of Chapter 3 address the topic of the learning climate, effective planning and readiness to learn.

The Church as Reflecting Community: Models of Adult Religious Learning, Loretta Girzaitis, Twenty-Third Publications, P.O. Box 180, West Mystic, Conn. 06388, 1977. (Paper, 8½ x 11, 186 pp.) Chapter 1 discusses the need for continuing learning; Chapter 5 addresses the topic of the community as educator with emphasis on the climate of the community.

"Motivation for Adult Religious Education," James R. Schaefer, *The Living Light*, Vol. 11, No. 3 (Fall 1974), pages 349-355. Schaefer provides a more complete description of the various kinds of motivation than is given in this chapter.

Motivating Adults for Religious Education, Kevin Coughlin, National Conference of Diocesan Directors of Religious Education—CCD, 1312 Massachusetts Ave., N.W., Washington, D.C. 20005, 1976. (Paper, 48 pp.) This NCDD research paper describes Coughlin's theory of the problem of motivation as well as many of the factors relating to motivation.

Adult Religious Education: The 20th-Century Challenge, Leon McKenzie, Twenty-Third Publications, P.O. Box 180, West Mystic, Conn. 06388, 1975. (Paper, 160 pp.) Chapter 15 discusses how to provide a climate for adult learning that will foster continued participation.

8.
Principles Of
Adult Learning

Much has already been said about what an adult is and how adults learn. This chapter is an effort to synthesize and summarize the preceding chapters into a listing of principles for use as the foundation for planning and implementing religious education programs for adults. This listing is primarily the author's personal synthesis of much of the preceding material. Readers are strongly encouraged to analyze this section critically in order to determine their own principles for adult learning.

Principles

A. Adults learn best when they are treated with respect, as self-directing persons.

Children realize that they are dependent on others for many aspects of their lives. However, adults see themselves as self-directing individuals who are independent. If adults perceive that they are being treated as children or without respect (being talked down to or given simplistic explanations, with their questions ridiculed or ignored), they will not participate in such programs.

B. Adults learn best when the learning situation is related to their past experiences.

Because of their increased age and responsibility, adults have many more and different experiences than do children. This experience can be a rich resource for learning which the adult educator should try to tap and use in the learning experience. However, the added experience of adults can sometimes be a block to new learning if the experience has been such that it leads the adult to think there is only one way to do something. In either case, the adult educator should be aware that the adults have different experiences, should relate the content and method of the learning situation to the adult's previous experience, and should design activities which assist adults in becoming more aware of their experiences.

C. Adults learn best when they have participated in the planning of the learning activity and set their own goals.

When adults are involved in the planning of a learning activity, they make a greater commitment to participate, and their level of interest is higher. While it is usually not possible for all the people expected to participate to be involved in the planning of a program, it is important that some of the prospective participants be consulted or involved in the program planning to try to ensure that the real needs and interests of the adults are being addressed.

Adults can assist in setting their own goals through personal interviews, phone calls, surveys, etc. Early in the learning experience, the adults should be asked what they hope and expect to get out of the participation. The program should be explained clearly in the first session so that the participants understand what they are committing themselves to.

D. Adults learn best when they are physically comfortable and can socialize with those in the learning group.

Children can put up with uncomfortable situations much

better than adults because their bodies are more flexible. Because of the effects of aging, adults need more physical comfort, and hearing and vision are also increasingly important factors to consider. Moreover, adults appreciate and respond to the opportunity to talk informally over light refreshments as part of the learning experience.

A comfortable setting, breaks, refreshments, and opportunities to get to know one another are not just "nice things to do" but are *essential* elements in adult learning. Another way of stating this principle is: "The head can't absorb more than the seat can stand."

E. Adults learn best when they are with their peers, freely learning in groups.

Adults need to react to what they are learning with others. Even when a lecture is used, some opportunity for adults to react, question, and comment (preferably in small groups where everyone has a chance to react) should be provided. Reports of the group's discussion can then be shared, and the learning of each group can be shared with others. Question and answer sessions in the large group setting provide only a limited opportunity for this reaction because usually only the bravest and the most vocal have the opportunity to speak.

F. Adults learn best when there are opportunities for a variety of learning activities.

Adults have different learning styles and preferences for the way they learn. Because they have had more and varied experiences they differ from each other much more than adolescents differ from each other. Some prefer to learn through visual methods (newspaper, books, TV), others prefer audial methods (lectures, tapes), and some prefer various combinations.

Not only should there be a variety of topics, but there is a growing awareness that it is important to provide a variety of methods in order to attract adults. These methods could include some discussions, lectures, coffee klatches, etc., on the same topic.

G. *Adults learn best in a problem-centered situation, when a question needs resolving or when a task needs doing.*

Adults need something to get their teeth into. This is why reflection questionnaires or simulated problems are very effective in enabling adults to learn. Even when a lecture is used, the speaker should pose some problem which the presentation addresses or ask some questions for reaction and comment.

Providing adults with an opportunity to write something down (as in a reflection questionnaire with genuinely divergent choices to help adults sharpen and identify their views) is a way to have the participants in a group discussion begin from some common experience. It is also easier for most adults to verbalize *what* one has written down (or checked or circled) and tell *why* that particular response was chosen than it is to speak off the top of one's head.

H. *Adults learn best when they can see progress, immediate results and some rewards for the time they put into learning.*

Adults will not respond to the reasoning sometimes given to children that a particular activity or program will help them later on in life.

Adults, because of the demands made on them and their time, need to see immediate application and results that will help them either personally (e.g., grow in their own faith) or functionally (e.g., help them to be better parents or deal with a particular problem they are facing). When this is done, the success of providing immediate results is higher. The application of this principle is often challenging because many adults do not view their faith as an integral part of their total lifestyle.

I. Adults learn best when they evaluate themselves.

Because they see themselves as independent and self-directing people, adults often feel resentful when they perceive that they are being evaluated by others. Rather, adults should be encouraged to evaluate themselves through the use of self-evaluation questionnaires or by asking them to share in a small group what they have learned and how well they feel they have participated.

Some kind of reaction or evaluation method should be used at the conclusion of adult programs so that the reactions of the participants can be used in planning follow-up or future programs.

This list of principles and guidelines is by no means all-inclusive, for there are many other principles which relate to adult learning. But these principles do give program planners a basis from which to work in considering the presuppositions and assumptions that they make in developing a program for adults.

Some Questions To Consider

A. Which of these principles of adult learning have you tried best to apply in your previous programs for adult religious education? Which ones have been most lacking in your previous program?

B. What principles do you agree with the most? Why?

C. What principles do you find hardest to accept as operating principles for programs of adult religious education?

D. What aspects of your present planning methods and program implementation would have to change the most if you could fully apply these principles?

Additional Resources

The Modern Practice of Adult Education—Andragogy Versus Pedagogy. Malcolm S. Knowles, Association Press, 291 Broadway, New York, N.Y. 10007, 1970. (Cloth, 384 pp.) Chapter 3, particularly pages 49-53, summarizes Knowles' fundamental principles of adult learning.

Self-Directed Learning, Malcolm Knowles, Association Press, 291 Broadway, New York, N.Y. 10007, 1975. (Paper, 135 pp.) Though concise, this little book is packed with principles and suggestions regarding adult learning.

Adult Religious Education: The 20th-Century Challenge, Leon McKenzie, Twenty-Third Publications, P.O. Box 180, West Mystic, Conn. 06388, 1975. (Paper, 160 pp.) Chapter 3, "Key Concepts for Adult Educators," and Chapter 5, "Things You Should Know About Adult Learners," provide further clarification and explanation of adult learning principles.

9.
Developing
An Adult
Education Team

If it is to be effective, if it is to be continuing, if it is to be done according to good principles of adult learning, adult religious education in a parish must be the responsibility of many people. The pastor and parish staff members must be knowledgeable in the principles of adult learning so that these principles will permeate all of their involvement with adults. Liturgies, homilies, committee meetings and other events involving adults as the primary group should be based on good principles of adult learning.

But if adult religious education is to be a vital force in a parish, it must be someone's primary responsibility. Because adults have varying needs and prefer to learn in varying ways, programs for adults should be planned by a group of adults to insure that as many different views as possible are taken into consideration. Whether this group is called a committee, a task force or a team is not as important as the fact that there is a group which is responsible for the planning and implementation of the adult religious education program. The term "adult education team" is used here to emphasize the need for close cooperation in this effort.

Forming an Adult Education Team

The first and most important need for the beginning of an adult education team is a person who is personally interested in continuing religious learning and is willing to work with others in pursuing this interest. In his very brief but excellent handbook, *The Parish Adult Education Team*, Fr. James Schaefer suggests that, besides interest, two other qualities are needed by members of adult education teams: *representation* and *competence*. Various adult age levels and backgrounds should be represented. Persons with educational competence (such as teachers, catechists, etc.) and adult learning competence (such as business trainers or salespersons) should be included.

All these qualities need not be present in every person, but each person on the team should be involved because of *interest and representation* or *interest and competence*. If at all possible, a member of the parish staff (priest, DRE, etc.) should be involved with the adult education team. In Chapter 3 of her book, *The Church as Reflecting Community*, Loretta Girzaitis suggests additional qualities and skills to look for in recruiting members for the team.

The size of a team will be determined by the kind of parish and needs and interests to be met. Whenever possible, there should be at least four or five persons to provide varying talents and points of view. A group of fifteen or more will find it difficult to plan specific programs (a smaller planning team would be more desirable), but the large group could be very helpful in suggesting ideas and critiquing plans prepared by a smaller group. Smaller parishes may face a greater challenge in recruiting members, but there should always be two or three on a team to provide mutual support and variety of views.

Once a team is formed, the members should spend several meetings getting to know one another and sharing their convictions about what they believe and what their hopes are.

Prayer should be a significant element of these early meetings. An adult education team will not be able to assist others to grow in faith unless they are striving to grow in their own faith.

Moreover the adult education team should strive to deepen their own understanding of how adults learn and what the fundamental principles of adult religious education are. One possible way of doing this is to go through this guide in a systematic way to discuss what they see as helpful and to identify the areas where they need further information and study. The *skills' assessment* at the beginning of this book and the activity on problems in adult religious education at the end of this chapter should be helpful in this process.

The team should spend some time in determining their strengths and areas of need as leaders in adult religious education in order to determine the areas where they can resource one another and the areas where they need additional assistance.

Get Some Resources

Once a team has been formed and begun to function, it should acquire some resources. The resources listed at the end of each chapter and Chapter 11 in this book provide many suggestions which should give much assistance to adult education team members. An adult education library should be started if it doesn't exist, and certain basic resources should be purchased. An adequate budget must be available if the team is to be effective.

The team members should also begin to search for resources such as persons, facilities and institutions that will be helpful. Parish staff members are an immediate resource. Various members of the parish community such as teachers, administrators, business trainers and consultants, and people involved in publicity, advertising, communications, skills and human relations will all be helpful in planning and implementing programs for adults.

A major resource that should be thoroughly investigated is the diocesan media/resource center which usually provides books, films, filmstrips, tapes and a speakers' bureau. The diocesan coordinator or director of adult religious education should also be consulted for assistance. Meetings of the adult education team should be a rich learning experience for the members as they share with each other what they have learned from investigating what resources are available.

Interact with Other Parish Groups

In Chapter 2 of *The Parish Adult Education Team*, James Schaefer stresses the importance of integrating the adult education team with the parish structure. The adult education team is properly a sub-committee of the parish education committee, along with sub-committees for child and youth education. The adult education team should also strive to assist the parish council and other committees (such as the liturgy, social ministry and administration committees). The adult education team should not take over or interfere with the work of these other groups; rather, the team should strive to support their efforts and make them more effective in their interactions with adults.

The adult education team should make special efforts to share their learning with the other parish groups and to make periodic reports of presentations to the parish council and education committee about the learning experiences and approaches that are most appropriate for adults. The team must be especially careful to avoid the attitude that adult religious education is something "we" do for "them." Team members must witness to the fact that adults continually need to learn more in order to keep their faith relationships alive. When adult religious education programs are held, the adult education team members must be conspicuous by their *presence* and not their absence. If the team members are not present to participate in what they have planned, they will teach by their absence that on-going adult religious education is really for someone else—anyone else. Everyone in the parish will usually agree to the need for adult religious education—but for everyone else.

Plan Effectively

As mentioned in Chapter 7, one of the most effective ways of motivating adults is to provide excellent programs. Excellent programs require much planning and hard work. One of the most important responsibilities of the adult education team is to provide systematic planning and excellent implementation of practical programs to enable adults to continue their religious learning. Chapter 10 suggests some of the important questions to ask and a planning process to use.

Being a member of an active adult education team ought to be an enriching growth experience. If it is not, if the meetings are dull and boring, if the members come only out of a sense of obligation, then something is wrong. Hard work in itself is not necessarily boring or dull. Hard work can be interesting and enticing—when we realize we are growing and learning and becoming better or more skilled persons. So if meetings are becoming a drag, examine what is happening. Are the basic principles of adult learning (see Chapter 8) being violated by the very group that should know them best? Are the members unconvinced about the reasons for adult religious education (see Chapter 2)? If these or other reasons are the cause, the team should take time to examine its own growth and development. If learning can't be exciting and growthful for them, they will not be able to make it exciting and growthful for others.

Some Questions To Consider

A. How has the adult education team been recruited and trained in the past?

B. What approach do we want to take in recruiting and training additional members for our adult education team?

C. What are the major concerns and problems we will face, and how will we address them?

Additional Resources

The Parish Adult Education Team, James R. Schaefer, Division of Adult Religious Education, Archdiocese of Baltimore, 320 Cathedral St., Baltimore, Md. 21201, 1975. (Paper, 15 pp.) This brief booklet is packed with suggestions and information for beginning an adult education team. It can easily be read in fifteen minutes, and it provides many opportunities for discussion and planning.

The Church as Reflecting Community: Models of Adult Religious Learning, Loretta Girzaitis, Twenty-Third Publications, P.O. Box 180, West Mystic, Conn. 06388, 1977. (Paper, 8 1/2 x 11, 186 pp.) Chapter 3 discusses the issue of recruiting the adult education team, and Chapter 4 deals with training the adult education team. Both chapters provide much information and suggestions for discussion and action on these two important concerns.

"How To Start Adult Education." James R. Schaefer, *Today's Parish*, Vol. 8, No. 4, April 1976, pages 39-42. This brief article gives many concrete suggestions for getting started in adult education.

The Parish as Learning Community, Thomas Downs, Paulist Press, 545 Island Road, Ramsey, N.J., 07446,

Problems in Adult Religious Education

Listed below are some of the more frequently mentioned problems faced by leaders in adult religious education. Please rank in order the problems you experience in adult religious education in your local situation. Score the biggest problem you see as 10, the second biggest as 9, the third biggest as 8, etc. If one of the items mentioned is not a problem for you at all, put a 0 next to it. Feel free to add additional problems you are experiencing which are not listed, and include them in your ranking: 10, 9, 8, etc.

———— absence of well-qualified resource persons

———— lack of good theological and scriptural reading materials

———— disinterest and non-cooperation by clergy

———— lack of motivation on the part of adults to participate

———— ignorance of good program planning methods

———— ineffective volunteer group leaders

———— poor quality of published programs for adults

———— inadequate funding for adult religious education programs

———— lack of awareness of reasons why adult education is needed

———— uncomfortable or inadequate facilities for adult programs

———— lack of adult audio-visual aids

(write-ins)

———— _____

———— _____

———— _____

- Why is the problem you ranked as the biggest your most difficult to deal with?
- Who can help you address this problem?
- What approach(es) would you suggest in dealing with your biggest problem?

87

1979. (Paper, 119 pp.) This book was prepared as a resource paper for the National Conference of Diocesan Directors of Religious Education—CCD. It discusses at length various models of learning and models of parishes with suggestions for developing the parish as the context for lifelong religious learning. This is a very useful tool for helping parish leaders and committees evaluate their assumptions and principles of parish religious educaton.

Critical Issues, A Report on the Work of the Regional Consultants for Adult Education, Department of Education, U.S. Catholic Conference, 1312 Massachusetts Ave., N.W., Washington, D.C. 20005, 1977. (Paper, 8 1/2 x 11, 22 pp.) This report summarizes the major issues in adult religious education as seen by eighteen regional representatives who are intimately involved in adult religious education. The report also describes the approaches being taken to deal with these issues.

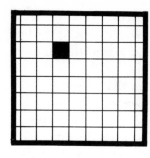

10.
Planning
Adult Religious
Education Programs

Once an adult education team has been formed and begun to function, it is important that the team plan adult programs in an orderly and systematic way. Before the actual planning begins, the team should spend some time discussing its assumptions about planning.

Do You Plan for Differences or Similarities?

We all make basic assumptions when we plan. Some people assume that the parish community is one large group with similar needs: thus, they plan assuming that everyone has the same, or very close to the same, needs. Others view the parish community as a vast sea of individuals who are very different from each other and rarely, if ever, have similar needs. The reality is probably somewhere in between.

It is important to realize that the older the age group one is dealing with, the greater the probability that the individuals in the group are more diverse.

So planning on the assumption that everyone has the same needs will not be realistic. However, adults within a community often have similar needs—though in different degrees. When we are speaking of needs of the community, it is possible to speak of similar or common needs. For instance, to celebrate effectively the sacrament of reconciliation according to the revised rite, everyone needs to understand the meaning and form of the rite.

In planning for adults, it is important that as many adults as possible participate in the planning process. This does not mean that programs should be planned by a committee of hundreds. It does mean that the planning *team* should consult others during the planning process to determine as best they can the needs of the anticipated participants, their preferred learning styles, and the topics of interest to them. The planning team should spend considerable time discussing some of the previous chapters of this book (particularly the ones on psychological development, andragogy, motivation, and principles of adult learning) to deepen their own awareness of the basic principles of adult education.

Questions To Ask in Planning

There are many ways to plan, and each planning team will develop its own style of planning. Whatever style is developed, there are certain basic questions to ask: In his book *Program Planning for Adult Christian Education*, James Schaefer suggests six basic questions to consider as a foundation for planning. The six questions are:

WHY? Why have a program of adult religious education in our parish? What is the specific purpose of this program? Why are certain needs being addressed and what goals and objectives have been chosen for the program?

WHO? Who are the anticipated participants in the program? Who are the leaders or resource persons in the program? What are the needs of the learners and the talents of the leaders? How will the needs and talents be determined?

90

WHAT? What content or topics are most appropriate for this program? Knowing the needs of the parish and the learners, what is the scope of the program?

HOW? How can the participants best learn the content? How can the participants be most involved in the learning experience? What learning activities will enable the most learning to occur?

WHERE? Where can the programs be held to allow the most learning to occur? What facilities (parish hall, meeting room, homes, church) will provide the best atmosphere for the kinds of learning activities chosen?

WHEN? When can the program be held to maximize learning? When are the participants able to be present? When are facilities available? How much time is needed?

There are many additional questions that can be asked, and they will naturally arise as the team plans. But these six basic questions provide a foundation for good planning.

A Suggested Planning Process

There are several good processes for planning, and everyone involved in adult religious education should be familiar with planning methods. Here is one planning process that has been found effective.

Step One: Discover the Needs/Interests: This step should include parish/community needs (such as providing for the catechesis for the new rite of reconciliation) and also individual needs (such as helping parents cope with the pressures of parenthood, enabling persons to deepen their own faith commitment, etc.). Gathering needs and interests can be done in many ways: surveys, personal interviews, observation, telephone calls, letters to a random sample of people, etc. When gathering needs, it is best to use as many methods as possible and consult as many people as possible. Once the needs are gathered, it is important to prioritize them—i.e., determine which ones are most important and then select three or four (or whatever number you choose) to try to respond to.

Without a clear definition of the needs and problems involved, there is a great risk that the program will flounder because it is not responding to real needs or interests.

Step Two: *Set General Goals*: After determining needs and interests, you now have some idea of the scope of the task you face. This is the time to set general, over-all goals which give direction to your work. The goal should be a general statement of the desired situation when a need has been met or alleviated or a description of the direction to be taken. An example of a goal would be: "To build up a spirit of friendliness among the adults in our parish." Set as many goals as you think you need or want to meet the needs you have discovered, but don't spend all your time discussing the wording of the goals or worrying about finding a goal for every specific need. Start with one or two general goals and work intensely on them, rather than have twenty-two goals and not do much on any of them.

Step Three: *Define Specific Objectives*. This is a crucial step, because goals give only a general direction and vision to your planning. Specific objectives are needed in order to realize the goals. The objectives should be very specific statements of the *actions* that will be attempted to achieve the goal. There can be several objectives for each goal, e.g., for the goal about friendliness above, the objectives might be: (a) to hold a dance during the summer to welcome new parishioners into our community; (b) to serve coffee and doughnuts after Mass one Sunday a month; (c) to establish a newsletter to publish names of new parishioners and announce baptisms, First Communions, confirmations, marriages, etc. The more specific the objectives are, the better the chances that they will be achieved.

To be useful, objectives should meet certain criteria. Good objectives ought to be:

Clear: The specific action to be taken must be easily understood. Those implementing the objective must know what is expected of them.

Specific: Good objectives spell *what* will be done, by *whom*, by *what time*, and at *what cost* (if any).

Realistic: Good objectives describe the next step (and not what is already being done) that is realistically achievable. It is extremely frustrating to be asked to do something that is impossible to achieve.

Measurable: For an objective to be effective, you must be able to determine whether or not it has been achieved. The actual means of evaluating whether the objective has been achieved should be determined during the planning process—before the program begins (see Step Six of the planning process).

The setting of good objectives is crucial to the success of the remaining steps of the planning process, and it is especially important if effective evaluation is to be possible. An example of a good objective is: "To conduct, prior to (specific date), a five-session New Testament study program for 120 adults in small groups in eight neighborhoods of the parish with a participant fee large enough to cover only the cost of materials."

Step Four: Design a Program. Using the principles of how adults learn best (see Chapter 8), design a program of activities to accomplish each objective. This program design should be detailed and precise. It should include: the program's goals and objectives; an outline of its main elements; methods of presentation and implementation; time duration; assignment of various tasks and responsibilities; funds and resources needed for the program; and all other information considered important to the programming team and those responsible for approving and sponsoring the program.

Step Five: Examine Your Resources. After getting a picture of the needs and interests that should be addressed, find out what resources are available to help you meet these needs. Resources include persons (look at your own parish community to see the talents and gifts of your own people), materials (books, filmstrips, films, tapes, study guides, etc.), facilities (meeting rooms, homes, methods of transportation, etc.) and money (doing adult education effectively requires money— just like anything else that is important and necessary). Look first at your own community to see what resources are available. Then find out what resources are available from other parishes/schools/educational institutions around you. At the same time, consult the diocesan education office to see what assistance is available there. Request a copy of the A-V Catalogue if you don't already have one. Look in every place you can, and ask everyone you can, to see what is available to help you meet your needs. The diocesan coordinator of adult education is available to assist you in all these steps.

Since resources are not unlimited, it is necessary to allocate the available resources among the various proposed programs. Here is where priorities have to be established in accord with the needs and general goals. Sometimes hard decisions have to be made in the light of real needs. It is important that the parish council and the committee for Christian education be involved with determining the major policies and setting the overall priorities which are used to allocate resources.

A vital element of this step is the preparation of a detailed *budget* for the time period of the program (usually one year). The budget becomes a major theological and policy statement because it clearly shows what the group considers to be important by the allocation of the various resources (personnel, facilities, materials, finances) to the various programs designed to achieve the specific objectives. All costs of implementing programs must be calculated as accurately as possible in advance. It is at this stage that the goals, objectives and program designs will have to be reviewed and refined, and possibly revised, to allow for the resources that are, or are not, available.

Because resources are limited, the allocation of resources reveals the choices made among the various competing objectives and alternative program designs. It is important that these choices be made according to clearly stated priorities and policies in the light of the *existing needs*. If the needs are great enough and if the program is good enough, then some major efforts should be made to find the necessary resources. This may require some creative thinking and informing those who set policies of the importance of the needs and the quality of the program.

Step Six: *Determine an Evaluation Procedure*. Part of the planning process should include the design of a method by which the program will be evaluated according to the stated, specific objectives. Evaluation takes place when a program is *submitted* for approval, while it is *being implemented* (by those *conducting* the program *and* by those *participating* in it) and at its *completion* by *all* those involved. The method of evaluation should be decided upon during the planning process and before the program begins. The program objectives should be the major criteria against which the program is evaluated: were the objectives achieved and how well were they achieved? If there are no specific objectives or if the objectives are too general and vague evaluation is difficult. Keep careful records of what happened during the program, what resources were used, how many participated, and what were the reactions of the participants and the leaders. To get an idea of this last reaction, some brief reaction form (if only two or three brief questions) should be used at the end of each session. A sample evaluation is included at the end of this chapter.

Now You're Ready To Begin the Program

You can see now how all the parts of this six-step process fit together. If it seems like a lot of hard work just to get a program started, *it is*, but the work pays off. It seems to be true that the effectiveness of a program is directly related to the amount of work that went into planning before the program started. Since it does require time and effort, it is important to plan with a team and start small. Doing one program carefully and intensely will bring greater benefits than doing many programs poorly and haphazardly. Going through a planning process such as the one described above helps everyone to keep his or her goals clearly in mind and to plan within the realistic limits determined by the resources available and the needs that exist.

The time spent in planning carefully for the program will enable those responsible for its implementation to act systematically and consistently. If changes have to be made because of unforeseen circumstances, they can be made in light of the overall goals and objectives of the program.

Refining and Recycling the Planning Process

Once a program has been implemented and evaluated, it is important to redefine the original goals and objectives. Effective evaluation will help you determine whether the needs have been met and whether the goals have been achieved. This information is helpful in planning future programs. Many times the same goals will be kept but the specific objectives will change. There will be times when new goals will be established because the evaluation process highlighted new needs and additional interests.

Some goals are continuing goals and should be part of the program each year. It is always important to determine goals in relation to the real needs of participants, needs which planners have helped to surface through their systematic approach to the adult education process. This information should be recorded and retained in a systematic way so that future planners can build on the strengths of previous programs and avoid the pitfalls discovered.

The planning process has been described in rather general terms. A specific example of each step would look something like the following.

Step One: *Need Assessment*. Through comments made to the priests when new parishioners register in the parish, the staff realized that the new people did not feel they knew many other people in the parish. The item "How well do you feel you know other people who worship at the same Mass with you?" was put on a survey mailed to one hundred parishioners. In addition fifty phone calls were made to inquire about this topic, and eighteen visits were made (three visits by each staff member) to discuss this with eighteen parishioners selected at random. The general result was that people in the parish did not feel they knew each other well.

Step Two: *Set General Goals*. The following goal was set by the staff in consultation with the parish committees: "To foster the building of a spirit of community and friendship among the people."

Step Three: *Define Specific Objectives*. The adult education committee defined the following objectives: "To hold a coffee klatsch with coffee and doughnuts and a speaker between the 9:00 A.M. and 11:00 A.M. Masses on the first Sunday of every month so that the people would have an opportunity to meet one another and socialize while learning about their faith."

Step Four: *Design a Program*. John Smith was asked to chair a subcommittee of four to six persons who would be responsible for doing the following:

(a) Make arrangements for setting up the hall.
(b) Purchase two additional tables.
(c) Secure outside speakers for the first two months and get parish staff for the next six.
(d) Use the sacraments as the basic themes for the presentation which should be informal and encourage small group discussion and questions.
(e) Contact local bakeries and doughnut shops to find the best prices.
(f) Put a notice in the parish bulletin each preceding week.

(g) Contact four parishioners each month to give out name tags, serve coffee, etc.

Step Five: *Allocate Resources*. The parish hall is scheduled for this event for the next eight months. Four people are lined up to set up the physical arrangements. The adult education committee members will take turns introducing the speaker. Thirty dollars per month is allocated from the adult education budget to buy coffee, doughnuts, etc. The adult education committee and the bingo group have agreed to share the cost of purchasing new tables. A member of the diocesan staff and a DRE from a nearby parish have agreed to be the first two speakers and parish staff members have agreed to speak at the next six sessions.

Step Six: *Determine an Evaluation Procedure*.

(a) At the end of each session, a half-sheet containing these four questions will be given to those who come:

How helpful was this session to you?
I was pleased/satisfied by . . .
I was displeased/dissatisfied by . . .
I learned . . .

(b) The chairperson of each session will write down the names of at least ten people who were present, and two people from each session will be called to discuss their reaction to the session.
(c) At the end of the eight sessions, at least ten people will be visited in their homes to discuss with them how well they feel the program fulfilled its objectives.

The results of the monthly reaction sheets, phone calls and personal visits will be used to write up a complete evaluation of the program to present to the committee for Christian education and the parish council.

Some Questions To Consider

A. How has planning for adult religious education been done in the past? Who was primarily responsible for planning?

B. What assumptions are you making within the adult education team about how you will go about planning?

C. How are you going to discover the needs and interests of the adults in the parish? What institutional needs of the parish should be addressed?

Additional Resources

The Church as Reflecting Community: Models of Adult Religious Learning, Loretta Girzaitis, Twenty-Third Publications, P.O. Box 180, West Mystic, Conn. 06388, 1977. (Paper, 8 1/2 x 11, 186 pp.) Chapter 4 provides specific suggestions for the basic steps of planning, and the entire book is filled with descriptions of many different programs that ought to be considered by planners.

Adult Religious Education: The 20th-Century Challenge, Leon McKenzie, Twenty-Third Publications, P.O. Box 180, West Mystic, Conn. 06388, 1975. (Paper, 8 1/2 x 11, 160 pp.) Chapter 7 suggests a process for assessing needs. Chapter 8 presents a seven-step planning process, and Chapter 10 discusses evaluation procedures.

Program Planning for Adult Christian Education, James R. Schaefer, Paulist Press, 545 Island Road, Ramsey, N.J. 07446, 1972. (Paper, 262 pp.) This book presents a comprehensive and detailed process for planning adult education programs and develops in depth the six basic questions discussed at the beginning of this chapter.

Planning in the Local Setting, Eloise Roth Rhodes, United Church Board for Homeland Ministries, Box 179, St. Louis, Mo. 63166, 1970. (Mimeograph, 8 1/2 x

11, 103 pp.) This is a practical yet comprehensive presentation of the theory and procedures of effective planning. The material in this booklet is concisely summarized in an eight-page pamphlet. *An Overview of the Steps in Program Planning, available from the same address. The Modern Practice of Adult Education—Andragogy Versus Pedagogy*, Malcolm S. Knowles, Association Press, 291 Broadway, New York, N.Y. 10007, 1970. (Cloth, 384 pp.) Chapters 5, 6, 7, 8, 9, and 10 all deal comprehensively with the various elements of planning and implementing programs.

Self-Directed Learning: A Guide for Learners and Teachers, Malcolm Knowles, Association Press, 291 Broadway, New York, N.Y. 10007, 1975. (Paper, 135 pp.) This book provides many suggestions to help a learning group design its own program of self-directed learning, and it includes many questionnaires and activities to use in the process.

Assessing Needs: Evaluating Programs, Catholic Education Center, Publications Dept., 251 Summit Avenue, St. Paul, Minn. 55102. (Paper, 187 pp.) This is a collection of sample surveys and evaluation forms which can serve as aids to planning teams.

Parish Adult Educators Expansion Handbook, Institute for Continuing Education, 305 Michigan Avenue, Detroit, Mich. 48226. (Large looseleaf binder, 8 1/2 x 11, 300+pp.) This comprehensive resource provides information about the adult learner, the parish team, program design, organization and administration, resources and other topics. Audio tapes to accompany the manual are available for an additional cost.

Adult Catechesis: Basic Parish Programs, Marie and Brennan Hill, St. Mary's College Press, Winona, Minn. 55987, 1977. (Paper, 8 1/2 x 11, 94 pp.) This book provides excellent suggestions for specific programs in adult religious education (such as a course in morality or a renewal day for married couples). This is an excellent resource for planners to use in the program design (step four) after needs have been assessed and goals and objectives have been determined. Planners should avoid the temptation to use this book to plan a program without doing thorough needs assessment to see if the specific programs suggested are actually the ones desired by the prospective learners.

Creative Learning for Adults: The Why/How/Now of Games and Exercises, Leon McKenzie, Twenty-Third Publications, P.O. Box 180, West Mystic, Conn. 06388, 1977. (Paper, 8 1/2 x 11, 191 pp.) This book presents the theory of why simulation games are appropriate learning strategies for adults as well as ten different games and samples of all the materials needed, which can be easily reproduced. There is also a chapter on how to design your own games. This book should be quite helpful in designing specific sessions or activities of adult programs, but some adults who see education from a more traditional perspective may need some "unfreezing" before they are comfortable with these activities.

Adult Education Procedures: A Handbook of Tested Patterns For Effective Participation, Paul Bergevin *et al.*, Seabury Press, 815 Second Ave., New York, N.Y. 10017, 1963. (Paper, 245 pp.) This book describes a wide variety of techniques and strategies for adults and explains the advantages, disadvantages and best uses for each.

Filmstrip

Adult Christian Education, Leon McKenzie, Alba House Communications, Canfield, Ohio 44406, 1975. (70 frames.) This filmstrip suggests a specific approach for planning, organizing and implementing an adult Christian education program for group discussion.

(SAMPLE) REACTION SHEET

1. I feel that this session was (circle one):

   very   somewhat   not very   not at all
   helpful   helpful   helpful   helpful

2. I was pleased by/with:

   _____

   _____

   _____

   _____

   _____

3. I was disappointed or dissatified by/with:

   _____

   _____

   _____

   _____

   _____

4. I learned:

   _____

   _____

   _____

   _____

   _____

(Please use the back to give any further comments or reactions.)

**THANK YOU FOR PARTICIPATING AND FOR COMPLETING THIS
REACTION SHEET**

(SAMPLE) EVALUATION

Adult Education Program

1. What is your overall feeling after participating in this program? [Circle the one(s) that most apply.]

   Enthused   Astounded   Satisfied   Indifferent   Ambivalent
   Irritated   Uneasy   Threatened   Angry   Discouraged

2. What did you hope to gain from participating in this program?

3. How well were your expectations fulfilled?

   ——— Completely   ——— Mostly   ——— Partially   ——— Not at all

4. How do you feel about the amount of presentation and the amount of discussion in this session?

   ——— Too much presentation   ——— Too much discussion   — A good mixture

5. Benefits and learnings that I gained from this session include:

   _____

   _____

6. Disappointments and dissatisfactions I experienced at this session include:

   _____

   _____

7. How do you rate the physical facilities?

   ——— Fine   ——— Good   ——— Okay   ——— Poor

8. How do you rate the length of the session?

   ——— Too long   ——— Too short   ——— About right

9. Some suggestions I'd like to make . . . (areas of interest I'd like to pursue; problems I'd like to solve; skills I'd like to develop; ways of improving future programs.)

   (Please use the back to give any further comments or reactions.)

THANK YOU FOR PARTICIPATING AND FOR COMPLETING THIS EVALUATION SHEET

Cassette Tape

CARE: Contemporary Adult Religious Education, Leon McKenzie, N.C.R. Cassettes, P.O. Box 281, Kansas City, Mo. 64141, 1976. (National Catholic Reporter Publishing Co., 4 cassettes, 3 hours.) These talks deal with the topics of determining adults' needs and interests, promoting adult education programs, encouraging adults to remain in programs and motivating adults to participate in future programs. The first cassette describes in detail a two-stage process for doing a parish survey as part of a needs' assessment, and the last cassette deals with the role of the parish adult educator.

11.

Some Activities, Resources And Programs

Having examined the planning process and the other important elements to consider in implementing adult religious education programs, it may be helpful to look at some particular activities, resources and programs.

Settings for Adult Education

In the past, when adult religious education was mentioned, most people immediately thought of a "class" or lecture or lecture series. These methods have been, and can be, effective means of adult learning, but they are by no means the only ones. Teams planning adult religious education programs should consider as many different kinds of learning activities as possible and choose the ones that are most conducive to the kind of learning desired. For example, to enable adults to learn more about the most recent theory of the resurrection by a prominent theologian, a lecture and discussion may be the most effective method. Many of the participants may have only a limited knowledge of the theologian's work and would therefore need some input before they could discuss the theory meaningfully. Keep in mind, however, that there may be limited interest in such a topic to begin with.

On the other hand, if the purpose of a particular program

is to enable adults to better understand their relationship with God as one of friend, having small "buzz groups" at the beginning of a session to allow the participants the opportunity to share their own ideas of what friendship means and their experience of how God has touched them through friends can be very effective.

The following list of possible kinds of learning activities is given as a stimulus to adult education teams to consider in their planning. The list is by no means exclusive or exhaustive, and several different activities ought to be used in the same session to respond to Principle F in Chapter 8 which suggests that adults learn best when there is a variety of learning activities.

Panel discussion	Committee round table sharing
Lecture/discussion	Films/filmstrips/discussion
Multimedia presentation (slides and tapes)	Fishbowl discussion
Coffee klatches	Buzz groups
Interviews	Simulation games
Role-playing	Reflection/sharing questionnaires
Shared prayer sessions	Home discussion groups
Field trips	Action projects
General forum	Dyad-Quartets-Octets-Sharing Groups

An Example

Let's suppose you are planning to have an evening for adults with the topic "A Modern Understanding of Grace." One possible way of structuring such an evening would be the following.

Introduction: After welcoming the people at the door as they arrive and asking them to make and wear name tags, the coordinator of the program could introduce the speaker.

Buzz Groups:

The leader would ask each person to think about and write down a sentence in response to these two questions:
  (a) When have you been enabled to grow through the involvement of another person?

106

(b) If you had to explain "grace" to a teenager, what would you say?

After three or four minutes of silent reflection and writing, the speaker would ask the participants to gather in groups of three to share their responses for ten minutes. This enables the participants to surface their own ideas about grace and learn from one another while providing the context for the speaker's presentation.

Reports: The speaker could ask some or all (depending on the number of groups) to give a one-minute summary of their discussion.

Presentation: The speaker then gives a presentation about the historical development of the meaning of grace with emphasis on the meaning of grace as a way of describing God's involvement and power in our lives.

Fishbowl Discussion: Six participants and the speaker then discuss the implications of what the speaker said for their own understanding and living of their faith in daily life.

Questions/Responses: The speaker could then respond to questions from the group.

Prayer Experience: Using the Scripture passage John 15:9-17 ("I now call you friends") and a slide presentation, the participants can be invited to pray in gratitude for the power of God in their lives.

The possible combination of learning activities in an effective program is limitless. For additional suggestions for choosing or designing learning activities refer to the following resources.

Adult Education Procedures: A Handbook of Tested Patterns for Effective Participation. Paul Bergevin, Dwight Morris and Robert Smith, Seabury Press, 815 Second Avenue, New York, N.Y. 10017, 1963. (Paper, 245 pp.) This book is packed with numerous suggestions for settings and activities that promote adult learnings.

The Modern Practice of Adult Education: Andragogy Versus Pedagogy, Malcolm Knowles, Association Press, 291 Broadway, New York, N.Y. 10007, 1970. (Cloth, 384 pp.) Chapter 7 suggests many formats and activities to use in designing a comprehensive program for adults, and Chapter 11, particularly page 294, suggests ways of matching learning techniques with desired outcomes.

Adult Religious Education: The 20th-Century Challenge, Leon McKenzie, Twenty-Third Publications, P.O. Box 180, West Mystic, Conn. 06388, 1975. (Paper, 8 1/2 x 11, 160 pp.) Chapters 16 and 17 present several techniques for adult learning.

Creative Learning for Adults: The Why/How/Now of Games and Exercises, Leon McKenzie, Twenty-Third Publications, P.O. Box 180, West Mystic, Conn. 06388, 1977. (Paper, 8 1/2 x 11, 191 pp.) This book presents the theory for using and designing simulation games to stimulate adult learning and also gives eight different games which can be used by adults.

Resources for Adult Religious Education

This book has provided lists of resources after each chapter in order to give immediate references to the ideas and materials discussed. Resources for adult religious education are growing rapidly. Often the problem is not that resources are not available, but rather to sort through the available resources to find those most helpful for one's local situation. Most of the references listed in the previous chapters will refer the reader to many resources. This section will list some of the most helpful resources as well as resources that were not listed in any of the previous chapters.

What You Should Get First

The resources listed here are the ones this author recommends for adult education teams to purchase first in beginning their work of planning and implementing adult religious education programs.

The Church as Reflecting Community: Models of Adult Religious Learning, Loretta Girzaitis, Twenty-Third Publications, P.O. Box 180, West Mystic, Conn. 06388, 1977. (Paper, 8 1/2 x 11, 186 pp.) If the author had to recommend one book for adult education teams to get, this would be the one. It discusses the need for adult religious learning, stages of adult development, and recruiting and training an adult education team, and it describes many programs that have been implemented across the country. The book lists many resources, and it is worth getting for that reason alone.

The Parish Adult Education Team, James R. Schaefer, Division of Adult Religious Education, Archdiocese of Baltimore, 320 Cathedral Street, Baltimore, Md. 21201, 1975. (Paper, 15 pp.) This brief booklet is an excellent resource to give initially to volunteers who may be interested in being involved in adult religious education. It is brief so as not to discourage anyone and yet gives a clear picture of what it will mean to be a member of an adult education team.

Will Our Children Have Faith? John H. Westerhoff III, The Seabury Press, 815 Second Avenue, New York, N.Y. 10017, 1976. (Cloth, 126 pp.) This excellent book provides an overview of approaches that have been used in Christian education, description of the four "styles" of faith and suggestions for planning and evaluation of religious education programs in the future.

The Modern Practice of Adult Education: Andragogy Versus Pedagogy, Malcolm Knowles, Association Press, 291 Broadway, New York, N.Y. 10007. (Cloth, 384 pp.) This is probably the most comprehensive single book on adult education. Though not written specifically for adult *religious* education, it is most helpful for understanding the theory of andragogy and the differences between other-directed learning and self-directed learning. The book includes discussions of assessing needs and interests, setting objectives, designing programs and evaluating programs.

Adult Religious Education: The 20th-Century Challenge, Leon McKenzie, Twenty-Third Publications, P.O. Box 180, West Mystic, Conn. 06388, 1975, (Paper, 8 1/2 x 11, 160 pp.) Leon McKenzie gives a practical yet comprehensive overview of the major authors and principles in adult education with suggestions for planning, organizing groups and the elements involved in enabling adult religious learning.

Other Helpful Resources on Adult Education

These are resources that have not yet been listed in this book that will also be helpful to those involved in planning and implementing adult religious education programs.

Future Shapes of Adult Religious Education, Marie Agnew, Paulist Press, 545 Island Road, Ramsey, N.J. 07446, 1976. (Paper, 8 1/2 x 11, 259 pp.) This is a futuristic study of the possible shapes and problems in the development of adult education.

How To Improve Adult Education in Your Church, Jerold W. Apps, Augsburg Publishing House, Minneapolis, Minn. 55415, 1972. (Paper, 110 pp.) This book provides guidelines for understanding the adult learner, for setting up programs and for choosing appropriate approaches and materials.

How Adults Learn, J. R. Kidd, Association Press, 291 Broadway, New York, N.Y. 10007, rev. ed., 1973. (Cloth, 319 pp.) This is a good overview of various theories and methods of adult learning, covering the major authors in the field.

SELF-ASSESSMENT

Use this page to assess your knowledge and skills as a leader in adult religious education. Read down the list on the left hand side and evaluate your own ability in that area by checking one of the boxes on the right. This will give you a quick overview of the areas you feel you are strong in and where you need further growth.

KNOWLEDGE OR SKILL	Self-Rating				
	Don't Know	Poor	Fair	Good	Strong
1. Understanding how adults learn.					
2. Competence in using adult methods of learning (andragogy).					
3. Knowledge of contemporary theology and religious education.				✓	
4. Ability to facilitate group learning with adults.			✓		
5. Understanding and skill in using effective planning methods.		✓			
6. Awareness and understanding of reasons why adult religious education is necessary for the Christian community.					✓
7. Ability to motivate adults to continue their religious learning.				✓	
8. Ability to set general goals and specific learning objectives.		✓			
9. Ability to choose learning activities that are most compatible with the content of the learning topic.					
10. Facility to interact with adults in a dialogical manner.			✓		
11. Expertise in administering and implementing adult education programs.		✓			
12. Familiarity with current resources (media, visual materials, books, etc.) for adults.	✓				
13. Understanding the stages of psychological development.	✓				
14. Understanding the stages of faith development.	✓				
OTHER SKILLS which you feel are needed by adult religious education leaders:					
15.					
16.					

This book attempts to deal with many of these areas. A quick look at the Table of Contents will allow you to go directly to the chapters you may want to read first or spend more time on.

aged to react to it, disagree with it, and add to it in order to sharpen and develop their own understanding and skills in adult religious education. May those who use this resource experience as much learning and satisfaction as the author did in preparing it.

BEFORE YOU START READING
USE SELF-ASSESSMENT
ON PAGE 3

The Adult Learner: A Neglected Species, Malcolm S. Knowles, Gulf Publishing Co., Box 2608, Houston, Tex. 77001, 1973. (Cloth, 198 pp.) This book provides a brief review of traditional learning theories, which are mainly child-centered, and describes at greater length the emerging theories of adult learning.

The Resource Guide for Adult Religious Education, The National Catholic Reporter Publishing Co. Inc., P.O. Box 281, Kansas City, Mo. 64141, rev. ed., 1975. (Paper, 8 1/2 x 11, 208 pp.) This book lists numerous books, tapes, films, etc., which are arranged under twenty-seven different topics.

PACE (Professional Approaches for Christian Educators), edited by Mary Perkins Ryan and Sheila Moriarty O'Fahey, St. Mary's College Press, Winona, Minn. 55987, 1977. (Looseleaf binder, 8 1/2 x 11, monthly supplements.) This is a resource booklet which is added to monthly, giving models and suggestions and theory regarding many areas of religious education. It is now in its tenth year of service to Christian educators.

Catholic Update, edited by Jack Wintz, O.F.M., St. Anthony Messenger, 1615 Republic Street, Cincinnati, Ohio 45210. (Monthly four-page format, 8 1/2 x 11.) Brief, clear style which can serve as a stimulus for discussion groups and other adult activities.

Published Programs

Some excellent programs for parish adult religious education have already been published.

GIFT: Growth In Faith Together, by James R. Schaefer, Paulist Press, 545 Island Road, Ramsey, N.J. 07446, 1973. (Paper, 8 1/2 x 11, looseleaf binder format.) This is a total parish renewal program with emphasis on catechetical and liturgical renewal involving all members of a local church community. The program includes three phases: *research* (a survey is used to discover attitudes and beliefs); *reflection* (persons are invited to meet in homes to discuss their concerns); and *response* (a comprehensive program of educational and liturgical events to respond to the concerns raised by the participants).

Genesis 2, Intermedia Foundation, 233 Wilshire Blvd., #305, Santa Monica, Cal. 90401, 1975. (Looseleaf binder format, 8 1/2 x 11, includes cassette tapes and six films.) This is a multi-media program for adult spiritual growth. It is designed for small groups (8-15 persons) who meet regularly. The program provides six films, audio cassettes, discussion activities and sharing exercises. The program is based on the work of Father Vincent Dwyer on spiritual growth and development.

Other Programs Involving Adults

Parishes are encouraged to investigate and take advantage of programs for adults that are planned and implemented on a wider basis, such as the diocese. The following can be very helpful in supplementing a parish program for adult religious education.

Cursillo: This is a weekend experience (Thursday evening to Sunday afternoon) for adults led by a team of 10-12 lay and religious leaders. The program involves talks, discussions, liturgy and prayer experiences for the purpose of building a spirit of community. The program is highly structured and has specific goals of deepening one's belief in oneself, Jesus and the community. At times the program has suffered from an over-emphasis on secrecy (which is not inherent to the program) by some over-zealous promoters of the program.

Marriage Encounter: This is a two and one half day experience of sharing for married couples. The weekend is usually led by a team of three couples and a priest. The basic format involves a presentation by team members, with individual reflection written in notebooks, and then husband and wife share with each other what they have written. The emphasis is on improving communication within the marriage relationship. Periods of prayer and worship are included, and the sharing is primarily spouse to spouse, rather than group discussion.

The goal of the weekend is to enable couples to grow closer through more effective communication. Because the program is so tightly structured, some leaders have tended to violate basic principles of adult learning by too strongly insisting on adherence to structure to the neglect of the freedom of adults to respond. When done well, this is an excellent marriage enrichment program.

For additional assistance in resources for adult religious education, contact your diocesan director/coordinator of adult education or the diocesan media/resource center. These persons and agencies can usually give immediate suggestions as well as on-going assistance in adult education.

Other very helpful resources would be parish directors or coordinators of religious education from your own parish or nearby parishes.

If none of these persons are available to assist you, get together with two or three others and develop your own skills by reading, discussing and using this book or some of the others mentioned in this chapter.

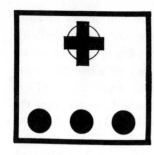

12.
Where Do You
Go From Here?

You've gotten this far, and you may be experiencing various feelings. You may be discouraged about the overwhelming task ahead. You may be interested but are not really sure you can do this "thing" called adult religious education. You may be enthused and anxious to get moving.

The Introduction mentioned that this book is "intended to be a basic and introductory resource for those responsible for and involved in planning and implementing programs for adult religious education." You may be saying to yourself, "If this is only the introduction, what will things be like when I really get into it?" Adult religious education is a challenging responsibility. This book has provided practical suggestions for getting started in adult religious education. Some may feel discouraged, but the author has tried to indicate clearly that involvement in adult religious education cannot be taken lightly.

When adult religious education is given serious consideration, people quickly realize that there are never enough people to do all the work, there is never enough time to get the work done, and there is never enough money or resources to do things the way you would really like to do them. Despite these reasons for discouragement, there has never been a greater need in the Church for a vibrant community of adult believers to make the message of Jesus a visible and challenging reality in today's world. And even when you have established a comprehensive program for adult religious education which is enthusiastically participated in by many, that will still not be enough. Most of the reasons given in Chapter 2 for the necessity of adult religious education will still be operative. An excellent program of adult religious education will discover new needs and new problems which will have to be addressed. Greater interest will be aroused that will have to be responded to. So there will never really be enough adult religious education.

Too many people in the Church somehow have gotten the idea (perhaps it was learned in some of the educational programs they participated in) that they can't learn any more ("you can't teach an old dog new tricks") or they don't need to learn any more ("I had sixteen years of religious training"). Such attitudes are among the most serious obstacles to developing a comprehensive program of adult religious education. But there is reason for hope.

If persons experience growth through participation in an adult religious education program, they will be motivated to learn more. Chapter 7 mentions the kind of motivation called "motivation by ignition" by which adults become aware of their continuing need for personal religious growth and work actively to achieve it. When this happens, and it happens ever so slowly, the number of adults involved increases. More resources are found. Greater enthusiasm is generated. Exciting things happen.

So it is important to realize the magnitude of the task, but it is also important to balance the immensity of the task with the realization of the possible growth than can occur. So it is time to consider if you are really interested, and if you are, it's time to *get started*.

But *don't do it alone*! Adult religious education is a group activity. Get some others involved. Be sure that you are experiencing enrichment and learning yourself. It's now time to get into that next book or that next meeting.

As you get more deeply involved in adult religious education, keep in mind the experience of St. Paul. Paul was an astute adult educator. In his first letter to the Christians who lived in Corinth, he spoke of the experience of being an adult: "Our knowledge is imperfect and our prophesying is imperfect. When the perfect comes, the imperfect will pass away. When I was a child I used to talk like a child, think like a child, reason like a child. When I became a man (an adult) I put childish ways aside. Now we see indistinctly, as in a mirror; then we shall see face to face. My knowledge is imperfect now; then I shall know even as I am known. There are in the end three things that last: faith, hope and love, and the greatest of these is love" (1 Corinthians 13:9-13).

St. Paul realized that being an adult does not mean that one has all the answers. Being an adult means being a self-directing person who is concerned about others and who realizes one's continual need for ever more growth. That's why, when it comes to adult religious education, there is *never enough* . . . keep growing and learning!